Hg2 Beirut

A Hedonist's guide to
Beirut

BY Ramsay Short
PHOTOGRAPHY Ramsay Short
                 & Tremayne Carew Pole

A Hedonist's guide to Beirut

Managing director – Tremayne Carew Pole
Marketing director – Sara Townsend
Series editor – Catherine Blake
Design – P&M Design
Maps – Richard Hale
Typesetting – Dorchester Typesetting
Repro – PDQ Digital Media Solutions Ltd
Printer – Printed in Italy by Printer Trento srl
Publisher – Filmer Ltd

Email – info@ahedonistsguideto.com
Website – www.ahedonistsguideto.com

First published in the United Kingdom in June 2005 by
Filmer Ltd
47 Filmer Road
London SW6 7JJ

ISBN – 0-9547878-6-2

Hg2 Beirut

CONTENTS

How to...

A Hedonist's guide to... is broken down into easy to use sections: Sleep, Eat, Drink, Snack, Party, Culture, Shop, Play and Info. In each of these sections you will find detailed reviews and photographs.

At the front of the book you will find an introduction to the city and an overview map, followed by descriptions to the four main areas and more detailed maps. On each of these maps you will see the places that we have reviewed, laid out by section, highlighted on the map with a symbol and a number. To find out about a particular place, simply turn to the relevant section, where all entries are listed alphabetically.

Alternatively, browse through a specific section (i.e. Eat) until you find a restaurant that you like the look of. Next to your choice will be a small coloured dot – each colour refers to a particular area of the city – then simply turn to the relevant map to discover the location.

Updates

Due to the lengthy publishing process and shelf lives of books it is very difficult to keep travel guides up to date – new restaurants, bars and hotels open up all the time, while others simply fade away or just go out of style. What we can offer you are free updates – simply log onto our website www.ahedonistsguideto.com or www.hg2.net and enter your details, answer a relevant question to provide proof of purchase and you will be entitled to free updates for a year from the date that you sign up. This will enable you to have all the relevant information at your finger tips whenever you go away.

In order to help us, if you have any comments or recommendations that you would like to see in the guide in future please feel free to email us at info@ahedonistsguideto.com.

The concept

A Hedonist's guide to… is designed to appeal to a more urbane and stylish traveller. The kind of traveller who is interested in gourmet food, elegant hotels and seriously chic bars – the traveller who feels the need to explore, shop and pamper themselves away from the madding crowd.

Our aim is to give you the inside knowledge of the city, to make you feel like a well-heeled, sophisticated local and to take you to the most fashionable places in town to rub shoulders with the local glitterati.

In today's world work rules our life, weekends away are few and far between, and when we do go away we want to have the most fun and relaxation possible with the minimum of stress. This guide is all about maximizing time. Everywhere is photographed, so before you go you know exactly what you are getting into; choose a restaurant or bar that suits you and your demands.

We pride ourselves on our independence and our integrity. We eat in all the restaurants, drink in all the bars and go wild in the nightclubs – all totally incognito. We charge no one for the privilege of appearing in the guide; every place is reviewed and included at our discretion.

We feel cities are best enjoyed by soaking up the atmosphere and the vibrancy; wander the streets, indulge in some retail relaxation therapy, re-energize yourself with a massage and then get ready to eat like a king and party hard on the stylish local scene.

We feel that it is important for you to explore a city on your own terms, while the places reviewed provide definitive coverage in our eyes; one's individuality can never be wholly accounted for. Sometimes if you take that little extra time to wander off our path, then you may just find that truly hidden gem that we missed.

Beirut

Beirut's past has been more than a little chequered, from a millionaire's playground and host to a glamorous '60s jet-set, to a war-torn hell-hole synonymous with hostage-taking and car bombs. Today it has risen, phoenix-like from its ashes into an urbane and modern metropolis, returning to its halcyon days as a summer haven for the rich and famous.

In the '60s the city entertained such international luminaries as Richard Burton and Elizabeth Taylor who came to banquet on fabulous seafood and lounge on yachts anchored off the Corniche.

The good days began to disintegrate in the '70s after the PLO were driven out of Jordan, only to set up camp in Beirut. In 1975 the Christians and Muslims turned to full- out civil war which was bought under control by the Syrians at the request of the Lebanese president. The invasion by the Israelis in 1982, supposedly to set up a buffer zone in Southern Lebanon, precipitated the unrest that would see the country divided into different factions backed by rival nations, religions and superpowers. The bombing of the US embassy and military bases in 1983 by Islamic Jihad suicide bombers remains etched in the memory of many of us as a symbol of what Beirut had come to represent. The 'hostage years' of the late '80s saw John McCarthy, Terry Anderson and Terry Waite imprisoned in cellars around Ras Beirut while the massacre of innocent civilians caught in the crossfire continued.

The war officially came to an end in 1990; however, trouble still continued in Southern Lebanon as Hezbollah continued attacks on Israel and Israeli-backed militia, which eventually culminated in the massacre at Qana in 1996. Since then Lebanon and Beirut have been peaceful – save for a temporary blip in February 2005 when the former Prime Minister Rafic Hariri was assasinated in a massive blast in Downtown. This eventually led to international pressure for Syria to withdraw their security services in April 2005, leaving Lebanon free of foreign intervention for the first time in 30 years.

The war took its toll on the architecture of the city – many of Downtown's classic buildings were destroyed, while the old French Mandate buildings in more outlying areas had to be demolished. The city's regeneration has been mixed. Rafic Hariri's Solidere company has restored much of Downtown to its former glories, although some may quibble that it is now a little soulless. Elsewhere urban planning has been virtually non-existent and a hotch-potch of buildings has sprung up, interspersed with the bullet-marked shells of disused houses and offices. The ruins of the old Holiday Inn, towering over Downtown, remains a testament to the brutality and savagery of the civil war.

Today Beirut is as glamorous as it once was; in fact the city is, if anything, more vibrant than ever, with a plethora of fantastic restaurants, stylish bars and chic nightclubs that keep the Lebanese dancing on the bar until dawn. In winter skiing is just 45 minutes away in the mountains, while in the summer the beaches and warm waters of the Med are just a 30-minute drive from the city centre; alternatively the stunning Roman ruins of Baalbeck make a peaceful respite from hectic city life. Beirut is a city that offers everything to everyone.

0   1km

HAMRA

DOWNTOWN

JAMIA

RAS-BEIRUT

SERA

SNOUBRA

EL ZARIF

RAWSHEH

15

7

1

TALLET KHAYAT

15

21

20

23

3

8

2

WATA

22

MALAAB

3

DRINK

3.   Art Lounge

SLEEP

4.   Al-Bustan Hotel
7.   Holiday Inn Dunes
8.   Hotel Alexandre
13.   The Metropolitan Palace Hotel
15.   Mövenpick Hotel and Resort
20.   Royal Plaza
22.   Sheraton Coral Beach
23.   Sheraton Verdun
24.   Sofitel le Gabriel

EAT

2.   Al Ajami
21.   Mandarine

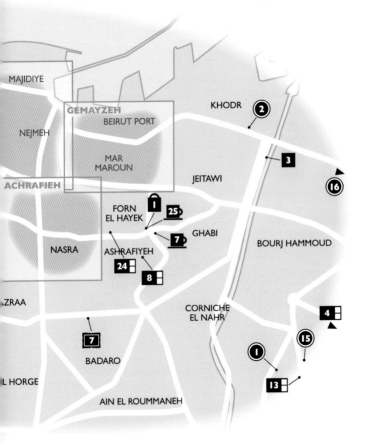

 SHOP

1. ABC Shopping Centre
3. BHV Shopping Centre
   Verdun

 CULTURE

7. National Museum
8. Pigeon Rocks
15. Janine Rubeiz Gallery

MAJIDIYE

GEMAYZEH
BEIRUT PORT

NEJMEH

KHODR ②

MAR
MAROUN

③

ACHRAFIEH

JEITAWI

⑯

FORN
EL HAYEK

🛍 ① 25☕

GHABI

☕ 7

NASRA

ASHRAFIYEH

BOURJ HAMMOUD

24

⑧

ZRAA

CORNICHE
EL NAHR

4

7

① ⑮

BADARO

13

L HORGE

AIN EL ROUMMANEH

 PARTY

1. Acid
2. BO18
15. Nova
16. Casino Du Liban

 SNACK

1. Amore Mio Café
3. Bay Rock Café
7. Chase
25. Watermelon

Downtown

What was once nothing but rubble, a no-man's-land of warring guerrillas and hidden snipers, is today the most prominent example in the world of a city centre rebuilt from the ashes.

Yet as one tragedy is built over and forgotten, another begins. The key player in downtown's reconstruction, Lebanon's assassinated former Prime Minister and major partner in Solidere (the company responsible for the rebuilding) Rafic Hariri, now lies entombed next to the giant mosque he built facing Martyr's Square. He was killed in a massive car bomb on 14 February 2005, by as yet unknown culprits.

What Hariri created in downtown has been both attacked and praised, but in the end what cannot be denied is that from ashes a vibrant city centre has been created with pedestrianized avenues and numerous street cafés and restaurants competing with a clutch of reconstructed mosques and churches.

Downtown, which consists mainly of boutique shops, offices, investment banks and parliament and government offices, has been criticized for lacking soul, being merely a touristic Disneyland for visitors to drink *arak* and smoke *nargileh* in the sunshine or cool of the evening. To be fair, during high season it attracts primarily that clientele with many Lebanese preferring to frequent the less touristy neighbourhoods of Achrafieh and Gemayzeh.

Yet for all the complaints levelled against it, downtown remains the cleanest area of the capital, with the least traffic (something that makes a huge difference in this town full of brand new SUVs and smoke-belching old Mercedes taxis) and wide streets coupled with ancient temples and ruins – including the Roman baths which sit in a garden beneath the government Seraille building. The old Ottoman and French Mandate-era buildings have been restored and some completely demolished and rebuilt making it difficult to tell the difference between the genuine and the faux.

There are numerous shops selling mainly clothes, shoes and jewellery and some restaurants, in particular the Lebanese ones, are well worth visiting. Look out for Karam and Al-Balad.

There are also a number of clubs and bars, which do a roaring evening trade especially during the summer months – Taboo and Baby M in particular are popular as is Beirut's version of Paris legendary lounge club Buddha Bar.

What downtown lacks is a major national museum of art, theatre or decent cultural space, something which angers many local people who ask how a new city centre can be built without thought for art, but merely for business and leisure. Still, there are numerous music festivals and random street exhibitions that happen in downtown throughout the year – check the Beirut Jazz Festival, which occurs in July as does the French Cultural Mission's Fête de La Musique.

Also in downtown is the recently inaugurated Saifi Village of arts located in the main residential part of the area off Martyr's Square. Here there are a number of new fashion boutiques, furniture and artisan stores and art galleries vying to create a mini cultural centre. It is, if not perfect, a good start.

With a few more years and more investment downtown will become a true focal point for the city but at present it remains one for the moneyed few rather than the majority of the city's population.

Once the reclaimed land next to the Beirut port is fully rehabilitated, a new park will be built surrounded by many new high-rise apartment buildings in an effort to create a modern and landmark skyline, downtown could really come to life.

A great place to walk, make sure to visit Martyr's Square where in March 2005 almost a million Lebanese congregated to demonstrate for independence from foreign interference in the country – the biggest protest in Lebanon's history.

CULTURE

2. Archaeological Remains
3. Al-Omari Sunni Mosque
4. St George's Maronite Cathedral
5. Jewish Synagogue
9. Robert Mouawad Private Museum
13. Arab Image Foundation

PARTY

3. Buddha Bar
10. Taboo
14. Music Hall

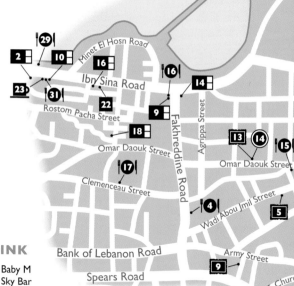

DRINK

4. Baby M
22. Sky Bar
23. Starlet

SLEEP

2. Bayview Hotel
9. Intercontinental Phoenicia
10. Intercontinental Le Vendôme
11. Markazia Monroe
14. Monroe
16. Palm Beach
18. Radisson SAS Martinez Hotel

SNACK

6. Casper & Gambini
10. Grand Café
13. Lina's
14. La Maison du Café Najjar
18. Place de L'Etoile
23. Sydney's

0   250m   500m

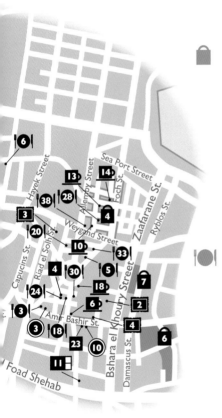

🛍 SHOP

4. Downtown
6. Saifi Village
7. Souq Al Barghout

🍽 EAT

3. Asia
4. Aziz
5. Al Balad
6. Balthus
15. Diwan Sultan Ibrahim
16. Eau de Vie
17. Fennel
18. India
20. Karam Beirut
24. Memoires de Chine
28. People Brasserie
29. La Plage
30. La Posta
31. Au Premier
33. Salmontini
38. Tamaris

Achrafieh

The neighbourhood of Achrafieh, in what was formerly known as East Beirut, is a predominantly Christian area filled with small streets and hotch-potch buildings constructed on top of each other. Situated on a hill that rises up from Gemayzeh and Downtown, Achrafieh has hotels, funky little shops and plenty of restaurants, bars and nightclubs, all making it an incredibly desirable neighbourhood to live and play in. Despite all that, it can be quiet at night, too – that is, anywhere away from Monnot Street.

The quarter also contains a number of churches, a theatre, galleries and antiques shops and a surprising amount of greenery in the form of tree-lined streets (although no parks – a facility that Beirut is severely lacking).

The buildings for the most part are old French Mandate period mansions and 1950s apartment blocks; there are also towering luxury apartments that have replaced former crumbling villas because land is apparently more valuable than architectural heritage. This has created a sometimes beautiful and sometimes unseemly juxtaposition – and has fuelled arguments over planning regulations and structures.

Perhaps off-putting for some, but interesting for those with a nose for old Beirut history, Achrafieh is built on the remains of the Roman necropolis, or city of the dead, which in ancient times was located to the east of the main Roman city centre. Within walking distance of Gemayzeh, Hamra and downtown, Achrafieh is without question one of Beirut's most attractive neighbourhoods, with a great deal to offer in terms of leisure and architecture.

On one side of the roughly square neighbourhood are Sassine Square and the ABC Shopping Mall, which sells everything from designer clothes to the latest electronic gadgets, and from sleek furniture to Starbucks coffee. On the other is the legendary Monnot Street, the hub of Beirut's new nightlife, with its vast number of clubs, restaurants and bars.

Hotel-wise there are the lovely Albergo and Gabriel Sofitel – both a departure from the town's otherwise functional accommodation – and the less distinctive Alexandre slightly further out; but all offer comfortable and attractive rooms within staggering distance from the most indulgent clubs.

The better restaurants are those located off the main Monnot drag, such as Al Dente, Abdel Wahab el Inglizi and Mayass, an Armenian–Lebanese delight. Bar-wise the places to check out are Pacifico, a Monnot instituion, and Time Out, for their individual charm, clientele and style.

If you want to imagine what the capital was like under the French, use Achrafieh for inspiration. Today, however, it bears little resemblance to the more Muslim areas of West Beirut, and has adopted a somewhat laid-back approach to life.

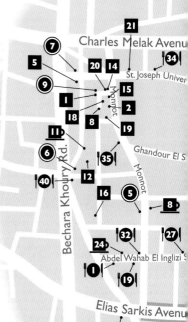

0   250m

Charles Melak Avenu

St. Joseph Univer

Monnot

Ghandour El S

Monnot

Bechara Khoury Rd.

Abdel Wahab El Inglizi S

Elias Sarkis Avenu

Damascus Street

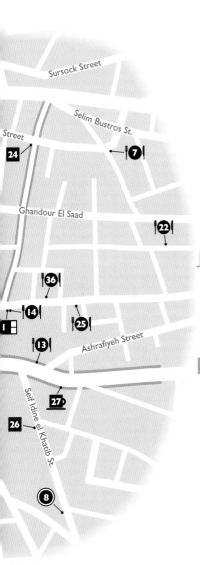

Sursock Street

Selim Bustros St.

Street

24

7

Ghandour El Saad

22

36

14

I

25

13

Ashrafiyeh Street

Seif Idine el Khatib St.

27

26

8

SNACK

8. Le Coffee
11. Henry's
24. Tribeca
27. Zaatar Wa Zeit

DRINK

1. 37 Degress
2. 1975
5. Bar Med
8. Celtic
12. District
14. Hole in the Wall
15. Ice Bar
16. L-Bar
18. Lila Braun
19. Moloko
20. Pacifico
21. Shah Lounge
24. Time Out (La Closerie)
26. Zinc

Gemayzeh

Gemayzeh is the Beirut equivalent of London's Shoreditch or Hackney, or New York's Williamsburg: a formerly run-down area close to downtown and central Beirut, with old buildings and cheaper rents. After the first trendy bar – Torino Express – opened in the summer of 2004, a spate of new restaurants and bars sprang up, making Gemayzeh the happening place for young hipsters and artists to hang in and shoot the breeze.

Over the last 18 months, this neighbourhood, slightly east of Beirut's downtown district, has rapidly fashioned itself into the number-one area to live, work and play. Unlike downtown, Gemayzeh was not completely destroyed during the tumultuous war years, and still retains the flavour of an old Beirut now lost almost everywhere else. Gemayzeh was populated in the past by many old, primarily Christian families, and today an older generation of residents still remains. It has now been designated an 'area of traditional character' by the Lebanese Ministry of Tourism, with its original red-tile roofs and buildings dating back to the 1930s and '40s French mandate days.

Gemayzeh is an enjoyable area to stroll through and soak up the flavour of Beirut. Halfway down Gouraud Street, there are the historic St Nicholas steps, a wide-open stairway leading up the hill to the famous Sursock Street and its ageing colonial villas and museum (recently restored by the Association for the Development of Gemayzeh). For two weeks every autumn the steps are taken over by local artists and craftsmen plying their wares in a local arts festival.

So far the area has managed its slow gentrification well, but how long this will last remains to be seen. As investment in the area continues to rise in terms of property and leisure service development – $50 million was spent on it during 2004 – some of the neighbourhood's traditional character is inevitably being lost. The Lebanese love to go out and they love to make money, and when an area becomes the place to be, anyone who is anyone wants a piece of it. As a result Beirut's wealthier, yuppy class is moving in at a rapid rate and those struggling artists are already finding it difficult to afford to live here as rents increase.

With three excellent art galleries, a plethora of jewellers, grocery stores, butchers and antiques sellers, mixed in with designer restaurants and bars such as L'O and Dragonfly, Gemayzeh is without question Beirut's most happening and dynamic neighbourhood.

During the day Gemayzeh's main drag, Gouraud Street, can get jammed with traffic, but you'll often see poets, film-makers, artists and writers scribbling away

on street corners or in local cafés such as Aweht Azzeiz (the Glass Café) or Le Rouge. At night it becomes a chilled bar and club district attracting a generally older crowd – leaving the teenagers to swallow up Monnot Street. It's definitely worth a bar crawl, hitting the different bars and trying the different specialist cocktails that almost all offer.

In the end Gemayzeh is one of Beirut's most picturesque areas, with good restaurants and interesting bars found nestling among the many old houses. Good both at night and in the day, it is well worth checking out – and it's within easy walking distance of both downtown and Achrafieh.

PARTY

12. Bar Louie

 SLEEP

17. Port View

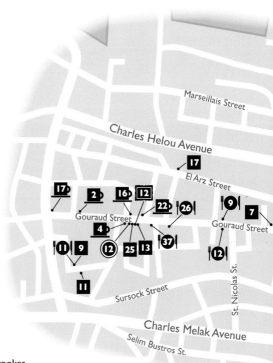

 EAT

9. Brookes
11. Centrale
12. Le Chef
23. Mayrig
26. L'O
37. La Tabkha

 CULTURE

10. Sursock Museum
12. Alice Mogabgab Gallery
14. Espace SD

0   250m   500m

Charles Helou Avenue

Street Al Nahr

Pasteur St.

14

23

17

10

J. Chader Avenue

Mar Mitre Street

SNACK

2. Aweht Azzeiz
4. Bread
16. One Stop
17. Paul
22. Le Rouge

DRINK

7. Biba
9. Centrale
11. Club Social
13. Dragonfly
17. Leila
25. Torino Express

Hamra and Ras Beirut

Ras Beirut, and the Hamra area in particular, arouse strong affection in most Lebanese. Older people remember the district fondly from their college days at one of its three universities – the American University of Beirut, the Lebanese American University of Beirut and the Lebanese Univeristy – all of which, but especially the AUB, have beautiful campuses you can stroll around. Students and young people see it as an alternative to downtown, which they perceive to be rather soulless.

But the area that spans the the Corniche and Ramlet el Baida at one end and the main Hamra block on the other remains a hub for shopping, hotels and businesses, a cheaper and more eclectic area than downtown (which took much of Hamra's business away when it re-emerged in the mid-'90s).

During the war Hamra was the centre of all intellectual activity in Beirut; its famous street cafés – Wimpy and the now defunct Modka, for example – attracted fierce political debate between artists, writers and all those outside the political classes. Today much of the debate has moved on to literary café/jazz bar De Prague and the small, smoky and very Arabic Barometre.

Always bustling during the day, Hamra has become the favourite quarter of Lebanese actors, performers and musicians, with two old cinemas, which have stood decrepit for 30 years, recently being taken over and refurbished as arts

and theatrical centres. Check out the Estral and Saroulla, located on the main Hamra high street, for their varied programmes of local and international performances. The Agial and Janine Rubeiz galleries both contain a large collection of works by both old and new Lebanese and regional artists well worth their salt. If art's your thing, go along and see what you think.

Ras Beirut also contains the upmarket shopping neighbourhood of Verdun, which fights to compete with the boutiques downtown, which has many of the same stores. Sanayeh Park, one of the few parks in Beirut – or rather a sort of concrete square with patches of greenery and trees layered around it – is located here, providing a pleasant space for a stroll in the sunshine. It's always full of families and an older, more nostalgic generation trying to cling to a lost Beirut outdoor life now dominated by the joggers on the Corniche.

Ras Beirut and Hamra retain much more of a Muslim Arab feel than Gemayzeh and Achrafieh, and bustle with street life, from shoe-shine boys to coffee and newspaper sellers. Although most of the architecture is modern and uninteresting, if you dig deep and walk around you'll find some attractive older buildings harking back to more picturesque days.

In the end, a stroll on the Corniche where the air is fresh may be all you need to get away from it all. It's more cosmopolitan here, and gives a truer impression of Lebanese life.

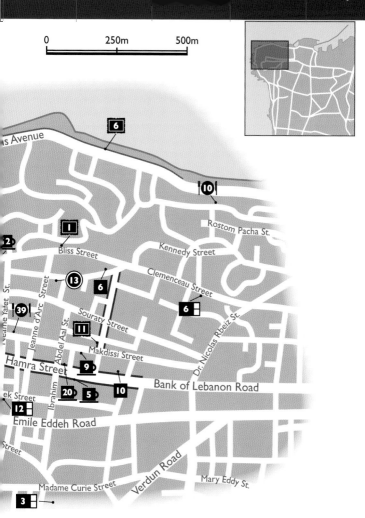

0   250m   500m

s Avenue

Rostom Pacha St.

Bliss Street

Kennedy Street

Clemenceau Street

Souraty Street

Makdissi Street

Hamra Street

Bank of Lebanon Road

Emile Eddeh Road

Madame Curie Street

Verdun Road

Mary Eddy St.

Jeanne d'Arc Street

Abdel Aal St.

Ibrahim

Dr. Nicolas Rbeiz St.

Neame Yafet St.

ek Street

Street

 EAT

8.	The Blue Elephant
10.	Casablanca
39.	Wadi Walima

 DRINK

6.	Barometre
10.	Chez Andre

sleep...

Beirut is a city that has once again become geared towards high-end tourism. As opposed to the city's restaurant culture, however, efficiency and luxury in hotel accommodation are more important than style or design. So while the selection is plentiful, few hotels are boutique or original. Owing to the influx of Gulf tourists in the summer months, the look and feel of the hotel environment is much more Middle Eastern than European chic. Because of the speediness with which the city has rebuilt itself since the mid-'90s, the emphasis has fallen on facilities, expense and convenience of location.

Of the 25 hotels included here, at least five suffered severe damage in the February 2005 bomb blast that killed former prime minister Rafic Hariri, but all of these have since reopened after complete refurbishment.

Beirut is not large, so wherever you're staying, the chances are your hotel will be close to major shopping, nightlife and tourist attractions.

The majority of the hotels are modern, some only a few years old. As the city has begun to attract increasing numbers of visitors, so the hotels have had to adapt and many have been renovated to extremely high standards. New hotels

have been constructed in recent years and big name brands The Four Seasons and Hilton are building impressive edifices near the seafront to cope with the continued increase in demand that's anticipated.

Yet what Beirut lacks is individually designed boutique hotels, so don't expect to lounge around in wonderfully renovated colonial villas or Arabic mansions. The Albergo, Intercontinental Le Vendôme and the Monroe all offer an escape from the predictability of chain hotels but don't have the same emphasis on uniqueness and design that has become the fashion in the West. Service, however, is something that most of Beirut's hoteliers pride themselves on, and hospitality is second-to-none. Most hotel employees are fluent in French, English and Arabic.

A couple of hotels have been included on the outskirts of the city because they have something unique to offer, be it the mountain air and panoramic views of the Al-Bustan or the opulent Arabian luxury of the Metropolitan Palace.

Room rates vary but most are fairly expensive. There's little of substance below $150 except in low season (Jan–May and Oct–Nov). In summer (May–Oct), finding a room can prove a challenge, so book in advance.

All the hotels included here have been chosen for their style, location and service and all include the basic mod-cons. Prices quoted are per room, per night, and range between the cost for a double room in low season to an executive suite in high season.

Our top ten hotels in Beirut are:
1. Albergo
2. Intercontinental Phoenicia
3. Sofitel le Gabriel
4. Le Meridien Commodore
5. Mövenpick
6. Intercontinental Le Vendôme
7. Monroe
8. Al-Bustan
9. Sheraton Coral Beach
10. Gefinor Rotana

Our top five hotels for style are:
1. Le Meridien Commodore
2. Albergo
3. Intercontinental Le Vendôme
4. Mövenpick
5. Sofitel le Gabriel

Our top five hotels for atmosphere are:
1. Albergo
2. Al-Bustan
3. Crowne Plaza
4. Sofitel le Gabriel
5. Intercontinental Pheonicia

Our top five hotels for location are:
1. Intercontinental Pheonicia
2. Markazia Monroe
3. Albergo
4. Palm Beach
5. Mövenpick

Albergo, 137 Abdel Wahab el Inglizi Street, Achrafieh
Tel: 01 339 797 www.albergobeirut.com
Rates: $250–950

The only true boutique hotel in Beirut, the Albergo is an absolute gem, located in one of the city's oldest, most picturesque and fashionable neighbourhoods. Opened in 1998, the Albergo is a converted city mansion with 33 rooms, and very French in style – not surprisingly, considering it belongs to Relais & Chateaux. It's total luxury. The interior décor by Tarfa Salam – from Aubusson tapestries, Persian carpets and Louis XIV dressing tables to Damascene wood ceilings and individually decorated rooms – remains teasingly concealed behind yellow stone walls. The service makes you feel like royalty, which explains its popularity with the exclusive clientele. Located near to Monnot Street and its abundance of bars and restaurants, the Albergo nevertheless takes you far from the bustling city into a well of calm. The rooftop boasts a small but exquisite pool and a delightful library-like restaurant that offers views of both the sea and the mountains. A beautiful hotel mixing East and West, the Albergo is truly a home from home, and French director Michel Chardigny is sure to keep it that way.

Style 9, Atmosphere 9, Location 9

The Bayview Hotel has just 36 rooms and sits right at the end of Ain El Mreisseh peering out onto the Mediterranean Sea. Close to the site of the bomb attack of February 2005, it managed to escape without much damage, and offers a more personal alternative to the majority of larger, more exclusive hotels nearby. Its particular attraction is its intimacy, which allows for almost one to one service. The rooms are plain, simple and tidy, so if you're feeling young, independent and up for a party, this is the place for you – not least because the roof terrace converts in summer into the C-Lounge, a house-music haven which opened in 2003 to a sun-baked crowd of nightlife lovers. Close to downtown and Beirut's historic ruins.

Style 7, Atmosphere 7, Location 8

Le Bristol, Mme Curie Street, Verdun
Tel: 01 351 400 www.lebristol-hotel.com
Rates: $215–800

French President Jacques Chirac, UN Secretary General Kofi Annan, British actor Stewart Granger and Crown Prince Albert of Monaco have all stayed at the Bristol in the last 50 years and, as you might imagine, it is a place of pure opulence (although you wouldn't necessarily guess so from the outside). The Bristol has classic style and glamour, and its 140 rooms are all decorated to the highest standards with some fabulous bathrooms. Located in Verdun, the hotel is a one-off, attracting an older generation for whom the name still has exclusive connotations. Still privately owned, the hotel basks somewhat in its reputation, but the service, for which it was originally famed, is still exemplary. Today it holds conferences and parties for Beirut's upper echelons, so be prepared to bump into some of the city's more establishment movers and shakers.

Style 8, Atmosphere 7, Location 8

Al-Bustan Hotel, Beit Mery, Beirut
Tel: 04 972 980 www.albustanhotel.com
Rates: $230–550

The Al-Bustan Hotel is piece of Lebanese history located high up in the hillside village of Beit Mery, and commanding a wonderful view over the whole of Beirut and the surrounding areas. Built in 1962 by the entrepreneur Emile Bustani, who died in a plane crash soon after, the Al-Bustan – which means 'the garden' – is possibly the only Beirut hotel to have an Arabic name and is imbued with plenty of Lebanese style, charm and authenticity to go with it. Still privately owned, it is clean and well kept; and while not as modern as the central Beirut hotels, each room contains a painting or sculpture from part of the Bustani art collection. This is the hotel to stay in if you want to be on the fringe of Beirut, and in the summer the mountain air makes it a cool alternative to the often-sweltering town centre. Just 20 minutes down the hill to Beirut, and about the same time to the airport, the Al-Bustan is an original Lebanese gem.

Style 8, Atmosphere 9, Location 8

● **Crowne Plaza Beirut, Hamra Street, Hamra.**
Tel: 01 754 755 www.ichotelsgroup.com
Rates: $215–2,325

The Crowne Plaza in Hamra is one of those places you might brush off at first as just another international chain hotel without much character – that is if you even notice it. Built and opened just two years ago at the Raouche end of Hamra Street, and slightly set back from the main road, this 21-storey building is the highest in the neighbourhood. The quality of the rooms combined with the breathtaking views from the upper floors make the Crowne Plaza a hotel to return to. Equipped with all mod-cons and laid out in dark mahogany, the rooms are spacious and modern. In the 20th-floor health club one can relax in a jacuzzi looking directly out onto a panoramic vista of the city, while the top floor bar/restaurant and pool commands the most attention with a 360-degree view of all Beirut. It's wonderful for a sunset cocktail.

Style 7, Atmosphere 9, Location 8

Gefinor Rotana, Clemenceau Street, Hamra
Tel: 01 371 888 www.rotana.com
Rates: $253–506

The Gefinor is located at the lower end of Hamra in Clemenceau Street, an older Beirut neighbourhood full of attractive Mandate-period houses and local artisan shops and stores. Constructed and opened in 2001, it is part of the small Rotana chain and features 128 rooms, a health club and great views over

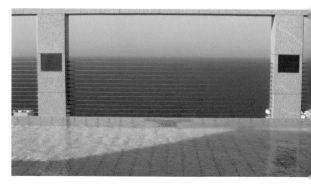

Beirut. Close to Hamra and Verdun and just a short walk to downtown and the seafront, the Gefinor is a sophisticated hotel boasting great service. Attractive rooms are modern without being too sterile, especially the suites, which compete with those of the higher-end hotels but at a much cheaper rate. The hotel's Trader Vic's bar-restaurant is well worth a visit for its food and famous *tiki-tiki* cocktails which are guaranteed to put you to bed early. Ultimately one of the highlights of the Gefinor is its rooftop infinity pool, in which floating feels deliciously decadent.

Style 7, Atmosphere 8, Location 7

Holiday Inn Dunes, Dunes Centre, Verdun
Tel: 01 792 111 www.holidayinn-dunes.com
Rates: $145–550

Located in the middle of the shopping neighbourhood of Verdun, the Dunes is more luxurious than most Holiday Inns. Its problem lies not in its service and facilities, nor its Beirut location. but in the fact that the hotel shares its building with a popular shopping mall boasting a four-screen cinema complex, a McDonald's and plenty of shops and boutiques. And that means lots of kids making you feel as if you are 110. Still, as a stop for a weekend visit, conveniently placed for shopping and the Holiday Inn, it has its benefits. With none of the pomp of the downtown venuesm it

doesn't really give one a good feel for Beirut – instead one could be anywhere in the world. If you like to shop or are travelling on business then the Holiday Inn Dunes is your hotel.

Style 6, Atmosphere 6, Location 7

Hotel Alexandre, Adib Ishak Street, Achrafieh
Tel: 01 325 736 www.hotelalexandre.com
Rates: $118–235

The Alexandre, named after Alexander the Great (who conquered Beirut), served East Beirut in the same way that the Commodore served West Beirut during the war as a haven for foreign journalists. Located in a secluded, green area of Achrafieh, a predominantly Christian neighbourhood near Sassine Square, and overlooking the mountains of Beit Mery and Broumana, the 197-room hotel has great views and spacious rooms. It was completely refurbished in 1997 to an international standard, but it is not particularly exciting in terms of design apart from a few original touches. What it offers is good-value accommodation and personal service. There's no pool, but you can enjoy full access to the exclusive and extremely fashionable St George's Yacht Club in downtown Beirut is available.

Style 7, Atmosphere 7, Location 7

Intercontinental Phoenicia, Ain el Mreisseh, Downtown
Tel: 01 369 100   www.intercontinental.com
Rates: $235–950

Probably Beirut's most famous hotel, the Phoenicia reopened in April 2005 after sustaining massive damage from the bomb blast that killed former Prime Minister Rafic Hariri. The refit has allowed the opportunity for the almost 500-room luxury hotel to update and become even more luxurious. Perfectly located for getting around the city, the Phoenicia overlooks the Beirut marina, which fills with exclusive yachts in the summer, and has incredible views of the Mediterranean and the mountains. The rooms, located in two separate towers above the hotel, are spacious and elegant. As part of a chain the Phoenicia lacks individuality, but that doesn't seem to deter the exclusive players who stay here. The service is attentive and the hotel offers every possible facility, from a fantastic spa to excellent restaurants. All marble columns and glittering chandeliers, the Phoenicia is the place to stay for its views, central location and high-class feel, but you will have to pay for it.

Style 8, Atmosphere 8, Location 9

Intercontinental Le Vendôme, Ain El Mreisseh, Downtown
Tel: 01 369 280   www.intercontinental.com
Rates: $230–780

Although part of the Intercontinental chain, Le Vendôme is a boutique for downtown Beirut. It's not much to look at from the outside but inside it is cosy, luxurious and lavishly decorated in a classical style; with stunning views over the Corniche and the Mediterranean. Each of the 51 rooms are individually decorated in different colour schemes while the 22 suites are furnished with old master prints, wood-panelling and heavy fabrics. There is no pool here, but guests may use the facilities at the Intercontinental Phoenicia next door, amongst others. One of the highlights is Sydney's, the 24-hour restaurant and bar on the top floor, a styled colonial English space filled with leather couches and offering great views. Come here late at night for an exclusive look into an otherwise hidden Beirut society. The Au Premier restaurant is one of the best in town, offering great food in high-class surroundings.

Style 9, Atmosphere 7, Location 9

Markazia Monroe, Syria Street, Downtown
Tel: 01 991 200 www.monroebeirut.com
Rates: $180–570

There isn't a single hotel in Beirut that can beat the Markazia Monroe Suites for location. On the edge of downtown, the 81-room hotel overlooks Riad el-Solh Square and is within easy walking distance of the shops and restaurants of Monnot Street and Gemayzeh. The drawback is the ring-road flyover running past the hotel, although it's not as noisy as you'd think. An extension of the Monroe Hotel, the Markazia is as modern as you get, converted from an office building and opened in 2004. Unfortunately the Markazia doesn't have its own pool or fitness club but guests have access to all such facilities at its sister hotel, the Monroe. All the rooms are spacious suites ranging from a one-bed to a four-bed, and come with every mod-con you might need. And if you're planning to stagger back to bed, you'll be hard-pressed to find a more convenient hotel.

Style 7, Atmosphere 7, Location 9/10

Le Meridien Commodore, Commodore Street, Hamra
Tel: 01 350 406 www.lemeridien.com
Rates: $225–700

The Commodore, the hotel of choice for foreign correspondents, had a refit a few years back when the Meridien chain took it over. The makeover has been sympathetic, bringing luxury restaurants and a dark, sultry, sophisticated feel to the place. Tracing its popularity back to the war years, when it was one of few hotels that journalists made their own in West Beirut, it was famous for its bar, where alcohol fuelled debate as bombs dropped – the Commodore has a deserved reputation for style and gritty glamour. The 204 rooms are comfortable but business-like, with some of the higher floors looking out over

Beirut's muddled urban roofscape. The Commodore is now the leading hotel in Hamra, with its chic, urbane style and low-key glamour. Unfortunately the guests no longer consist of grizzled, whisky-soaked journalists but more mundane tour groups and businessmen.

Style 9, Atmosphere 8, Location 8

The Metropolitan Palace Hotel, Horsh Tabet, Sin El Fil
Tel: 01 496 666 www.habtoorhotels.com
Rates: $190–2,000

This luxurious hotel opened in 2001 to great acclaim, and is part of the Metropolitan chain owned by wealthy Emirati Khalaf al-Habtoor. One of the tallest buildings in the city, it has become a

landmark on the skyline, offering fantastic panoramic views over Beirut from all of its 183 rooms. Very Arabic in style, it is expensively kitted out and has all the facilities you might ever need – including a directional finder for Mecca. The 1,000 sq metre penthouse on the 17th floor, the largest in the Middle East, is pure luxury. The central 16-storey atrium is impressive, as is the viewing elevator that disappears into the *trompe l'oeil* sky. The views alone make a stay worthwhile, but the down-side is a 15-minute cab ride back into central Beirut. On the other hand the Metropolitan is well located for trips to the northern resort beaches and mountains of Faraya.

Style 8, Atmosphere 9, Location 7

Monroe, Kennedy Street, Downtown
Tel: 01 371 122 www.monroebeirut.com
Rates: $150–600

The Monroe Hotel was completely refurbished after suffering huge damage from the bomb blast of February 2005, but continued the '60s theme in a contemporary style. Named after Marilyn, it is more Californian chic than Dubai glamour, and all the 101 rooms are simple and sleek. Located on the edge of Beirut's downtown, opposite the Phoenicia Hotel and overlooking the marina, it feels a little like an Andy Warhol museum, with miscellaneous items of '60s furniture and specifically commis-

sioned pieces of modernist sculpture dotted about. The two restaurants – Di Maggio's and the Peppermint Lounge – are pleasant places for eating and hanging out. But particularly of note is the bar-club, The Ivy, which is situated on the third floor next to the hotel's pool, and can be pretty raucous and decadent during the summer. Not good if you are planning an early night.

Style 8, Atmosphere 8, Location 9

Mövenpick Hotel and Resort, General de Gaulle Avenue, Raouche
Tel: 01 869 666 www.moevenpick-hotels.com
Rates: $200–350

Prominently located on Beirut's seafront, close to the Pigeon Rocks, with its own private beach and marina, two swimming pools and numerous chalets, the Mövenpick is classic luxury in the heart of the city. Owned by Saudi billionaire Prince Walid Bin Talal, it caters primarily to tourists from the Arab world, and offers unparalleled standards of service and numerous facilities, from stylish restaurants to a 2000 sq metre spa with 11 massage rooms. Opened in 2002, after many derelict years (the hotel was first built in 1975 but never opened), it has 293 rooms, the best of which have wonderful views over the sea. At night, the lights from the local fishing boats bob up and down in the waters in front of the hotel. The Mövenpick has a good Lebanese

restaurant in the form of the Bourj al-Hamam, which, given the sandy beach and a shopping arcade, make it almost possible never to leave the hotel at all.

Style 8, Atmosphere 9, Location 7

Palm Beach, Ain el Mreisseh, Downtown
Tel: 01 372 000 www.palmbeachbeirut.com
Rates: $150–740

The Palm Beach is one of Beirut's most loved hotels and also one of the most fashionable for the young, jet-setting crowd. Having suffered severe damage after the Hariri bombing in February 2005, it has been completely refurbished and updated. The 88 rooms are all tastefully decorated, many with four-poster beds and exquisite oriental carpets, and the suites are spacious if a little uniform. The Palm Beach's location close to Hamra and Downtown is perhaps its biggest selling point, together with the 360-degree views over the sea, the mountains and Beirut from the small, rooftop swimming pool. Adding to the overall feel of exclusivity, the rooftop fills with models and sun worshippers during the day, and party animals at night when the pool and the floor below become the legendary Sky Bar. As one might expect from the demanding clientele, service is impeccable and the Palm Beach has become legendary for its hospitality.

Style 7, Atmosphere 8, Location 9

Port View, Gouraud Street, Gemayzeh
Tel: 01 567 500 www.portviewhotel.com
Rates: $45–55

The Port View is a small, relaxed and refined hotel, and the only one located in the trendy Gemayzeh area close to the port and the fashionable local bars and restaurants. One of the cheapest hotels, its location is its primary selling point – it's quiet, and also reveals a side of the city that guests in the larger hotels do not get to see. The rooms are simple with basic double beds and private bathrooms, with none of the facilities and extravagances of the downtown hotels. There's no pool and just a basic brasserie restaurant, but Port View's beauty lies in its intimacy and the personality of manager, Mike Najm, whose knowledge of the city past and present is outstanding. It is an interesting choice for those not concerned with luxury and who would rather spend their cash on eating and drinking than a bed for the night.

Style 6, Atmosphere 7, Location 8

Radisson SAS Martinez Hotel, Ain El Mreisseh, Downtown
Tel: 01 368 111 www.radissonsas.com
Rates: $220–1,200

The Radisson is an intimate hotel, located in the backstreets on the edge of downtown, in an area populated by Beirut's infamous 'Super Night Clubs' (see Party). The spacious rooms, vast and classically themed indoor pool and fitness centre and friendly staff make it a worthwhile choice. Hidden behind the Phoenicia Hotel just a short way from the Corniche and Hamra, the Martinez is a getaway from the main hotels. The 185 rooms are simply decorated and functional; and it's this very unfussiness that makes it an easy place to stay. Retaining the chain hotel tag and its associated implications, the Radisson offers all you'd expect for those who know what they like.

Style 6, Atmosphere 7, Location 8

● **The Riviera, Corniche el Manara, Manara**
Tel: 01 365 239 www.rivierahotel.com.lb
Rates: $155–650

The Riviera is a 120-room hotel and resort located in the middle of the Corniche, close to the American University of Beirut. It's known in the capital as Silicon Beach because of the bikini-clad ladies enhanced by plastic surgery who populate the pool and resort area. The Riviera is an elegant, French-style hotel that would be at home on the promenade at Nice or St Tropez. The classically designed rooms are large and furnished with chairs and sofas embellished with intricate touches; most look out onto the sea and the yacht club across the road below. The Riviera is a popular hotel, especially in the summer when its mini-marina is packed with boats cruising the coast, and you'll find it's worth reserving well in advance. For water-sports enthusiasts, the diving club is one of the best in Beirut.

> **Style 7, Atmosphere 9, Location 8**

Royal Plaza, General De Gaulle Avenue, Raouche
Tel: 01 791 000 www.royalplazahotel.com.lb
Rates: $205–1,160

From the outside the Royal Plaza is not a pretty hotel. But then it doesn't need to be. Towering 12 storeys up, what it offers is a stunning panoramic view over the Mediterranean Sea and Mount Lebanon that's truly hard to beat. The majority of rooms are

suites offering space and a reasonable level of luxury, but they're somewhat lacking in terms of style. If you can afford it the Royal Suite on the tenth floor is a trick not to be missed: it has three bedrooms and balconies, and incredible views, giving you a feel of the city you don't really get anywhere else. The restaurants aren't particularly exciting, but the rooftop pool is possibly the highest in the capital and attracts a lot of toned sun-worshippers. The guests are mainly from the Gulf states as well as a few aircrews, so it's not the best place to be for those who want more of a buzz.

Style 7, Atmosphere 8, Location 8

Safir Heliopolitan, Australia Street, Raouche
Tel: 01 810 555   www.safirheliopolitan.com
Rates: $220–1,200

For a building that looks like a half-sliced slab of Swiss cheese, the Safir Heliopolitan couldn't be more classy – you'll find it standing high and mighty, set back from the Corniche sea road in Raouche. The lobby lounge area is an oasis of calm, with mini palm trees flanked by modern wooden fittings and leather sofas. Of the 144 rooms all but those on the lowest floors have sea views or face towards Mount Lebanon, which, in winter, with its snow-capped peaks, is a breathtaking sight. All the rooms are modern but not particularly spacious. The location is convenient for Hamra and Verdun, and it's a mere 10 minutes from the air-

port. It also offers almost direct access onto the highway leading south for those with an urge to explore the beaches and ruins outside Beirut.

Style 8, Atmosphere 7, Location 7

Sheraton Coral Beach, Jnah Avenue, Ras Beirut
Tel: 01 859 000   www.sheraton.com/coralbeach
Rates: $216–1,500

The Coral Beach Hotel is legendary in Beirut. It opened at the beginning of the civil war and survived throughout, becoming a haven for Beirutis who wanted to escape the destruction of their city. Today, however, it has suffered competition from newer more centrally located hotels. Opening up onto a quiet Mediterranean bay, it offers is a sense of quiet detachment from the city that few other Beirut hotels can give. The 97 rooms, all refurbished when the Sheraton took over the hotel in 2002, are spacious, modern and light, and guests can enjoy the sandy beach and a choice of two pools. The location, while quiet, means a cab ride into town; it's not far, but can involve an unpleasant argument with taxi drivers over the fare. Coral Beach's charm lies in its outlying destination, position and views, which make it very much a five-star summer hotel when the city centre gets a little too stifling.

Style 8, Atmosphere 8, Location 8

Sheraton Verdun, Saeb Salam Boulevard, Verdun
Tel: 01 803 804   www.starwoodhotels.com/fourpoints
Rates: $115–1,200

Opened in January 2005, the Verdun Sheraton is the newest
hotel to hit Beirut. Its owner, a wealthy Lebanese man from the
south of the country, wanted to bring a contemporary hotel to
the less-well-served neighbourhood of Verdun. Completely state-
of-the-art, the atmosphere here is one of sophistication and
comfort, with every available mod-con at hand. The 132 rooms
have panoramic views over south Beirut, the Mediterranean and
the Chouf mountains, and are decorated in a relaxed, boutique
style. Right on top of the Verdun shopping neighbourhood and
close to both Hamra and the seafront, the Verdun Sheraton
makes sense, especially if you don't want to break the bank. It is
surprisingly both a refuge and relatively fashionable spot to plant
yourself for a quick stay in town.

Style 8/9, Atmosphere 8, Location 7

Sofitel le Gabriel, Independence Avenue, Achrafieh
Tel: 01 203 700   legabriel@inco.com.lb
Rates: $162–467

We like the Gabriel. Although part of the Sofitel chain, it is very
much a hotel with a character all its own – which might, in no

small part, come from the personality of its owner, the flamboyant Lebanese rally race-car driver and wood-factory owner, Nabil 'Billy' Karam. With just 75 rooms, which is small for Beirut, the attention to detail is immaculate; each is decorated in an English style by London-based designer Nina Campbell, and comes complete with heavy carpets and upholstery. The Gabriel has a small indoor pool and health centre to help you to relax

after a day's shopping or to work off the excesses of the night before. The lack of a decent in-house restaurant is compensated for by the plethora of eateries of Achrafieh and Monnont Street, just 10 minutes' walk away. Friendly and hospitable, the Gabriel is one of the most charming small hotels in town.

Style 9, Atmosphere 9, Location 8

eat...

Eating is quite simply a passion for the Lebanese. Beirutis love to eat and love choice, facts that are reflected in the vast and diverse array of high-quality restaurants you'll find here. From French and Italian to Japanese and Lebanese, restaurants have multiplied in the last five years and, the trend looks unlikely to stop. Although many close after a year (or even less), those that do remain become hugely successful and maintain continually high standards.

Lebanon is a country where people generally begin to eat rather late – you'll find very few full restaurants open before 9.30pm – but there are several perennially popular places where you can eat a little earlier if you so desire.

Standards are consistently high, often with prices to match (especially if you are drinking imported wine). Lebanese wine is often delicious, but if this doesn't grab you go for the traditional pastis-like spirit, *arak* – which is a must with Lebanese *mezze* or grills.

With Lebanese food it is hard to go wrong. From simple vegetarian dishes of okra and rice, *hummus* and traditional flat bread, stuffed cabbage or vine leaves and *tabbouleh* or *fattoush* salads, to more complex and heavier meat dishes, the emphasis is on simplicity and taste. Essentially the main difference between Lebanese restaurants lies in their specialities, atmosphere and, of course, price. The best eateries tend to be located in downtown and Achrafieh, with a few more local kitchens found a little further out.

For more international cuisine, there are some great hotel restaurants, but the majority are independent. These tend to focus as much on style and interior design as they do on food, a trend that most local Lebanese restaurants don't follow. Consequently the décor in some of the top European restaurants is a sight to behold, especially when they sometimes find it tricky to shake off all traces of Arabian influence.

In nearly all the Lebanese restaurants and cafés you can try smoking a traditional *narguileh* (hookah) or water pipe. Sitting back after dinner puffing away on some apple tobacco with a strong black coffee is an extremely relaxing experience, and something that the locals truly appreciate.

French and Italian restaurants are extremely popular, as are, perhaps incredibly, Japanese. There seem to be more sushi joints in this relatively small capital than in Tokyo itself. Well, not quite... but you get the picture. Interestingly, however, none has a Japanese chef – most are imported from the Philippines or Indonesia.

Beirut's seaside setting means fresh fish and shellfish are constantly on the menu. The city's seafood restaurants come highly recommended and have managed to produce some quite exquisite signature dishes using the freshest ingredients caught the same day.

There are also numerous roadside vendors and bakeries that serve the traditional Lebanese take-away fodder – *manoushie*. This is a round-flat baked piece of Arabic bread, a little like a pizza, with a choice of different flavourings – *zaatar* (thyme) is the most common, but you can combine it with either *gibne* (cheese) or meat. These bakeries are everywhere, and people either eat *manoushie* for breakfast or late at night after partying.

Overall, eating is a serious business in Beirut, and the quality of fresh fruit and vegetables second to none. If you really want to try something exotic you can always go for the lamb's brain or liver, often raw, which are both popular Lebanese dishes for the discerning.

Prices given here are in dollars and reflect the cost of a meal for one with half a bottle of wine.

Our top ten restaurants in Beirut are:
1. Mayass
2. Centrale
3. Eau de Vie
4. Aziz
5. Au Premier
6. Al Mijana
7. Al Balad
8. Solea
9. Julia's
10. Al Ajami

Our top five restaurants for food are:
1. Karam Beirut
2. Mayass
3. Eau de Vie
4. Centrale
5. Abdel Wahab

Our top five restaurants for service are:
1. Mayass
2. Aziz
3. Yabani
4. Eau de Vie
5. Al Mijana

Our top five restaurants for atmosphere are:
1. Centrale
2. L'O
3. Solea
4. Mayass
5. Casablanca

Abdel Wahab el Inglizi, Abdel Wahab el Inglizi Street, Achrafieh

Tel: 01 200 550 www.ghiaholding.com
Open: midday–4pm, 7pm–1am daily $25

A large, glass-fronted Lebanese restaurant situated in a street at
the top of Monnot in Achrafieh, Abdel Wahab is popular for its
food, atmosphere and rooftop terrace, which is rammed with
locals and tourists alike during the summer. It has a deservedly
good reputation for its lavish Lebanese food served in ample
portions – order a selection of *mezze* (*hummus*, *labne*, cheese
rolls, meat pastries, *tabbouleh*), wash them down with a choice of
the finest Lebanese *araks*, and round off the evening with a *narguileh* (water pipe) – and satisfaction's guaranteed. Abdel Wahab
is loud and always full so remember to reserve a table. Go with
a crowd of friends for great food at reasonable prices in a hum-
ming atmosphere before you head off to the nearby bars and
clubs of Monnot.

Food 9, Service 8, Atmosphere 8

Al Ajami, Rafic Hariri Avenue, Ramlet Al Baida

Tel: 01 802 260 www.alajamirestaurant.com
Open: 8am–1am daily $25

Al Ajami opened pre-war and has remained open in West Beirut on the sea road ever since. It's typically old-school Lebanese, with comfy cushions and sofas are scattered throughout its pre-fab home overlooking the sea. Ajami is the place to catch up on local stories and gossip from the traditionally dressed and over-attentive waiters. This is the place to drink *arak*, smoke *narguileh* and gorge yourself on plates of *mezze*, *schwarma*, bowls of fresh vegetables and divine olives. The Arabic desserts are especially good (the *halawi* and *baclawa* are particularly sweet). The atmos-phere is typically vibrant, with lots of fun and loud Arabic music. Ajami is located in an exclusive residential neighbourhood far from the rest of Beirut's dining scene. When you leave, take in the coastal air and stroll down to the beach. You won't regret it.

Food 9, Service 8, Atmosphere 9

Asia, Riad el Sohl Square, Downtown
Tel: 01 991 919 www.ghiaholding.com
Open: 7pm–1am daily $30

A spacious rooftop restaurant (the roof in question is one of the national bank buildings) in the centre of Beirut's downtown area, Asia has incredible views over the city. The innovative design looks to Cuba for inspiration rather than the Far East, with mir-rors, low-slung couches and an abundance of wine and cigars. Asia's fusion cuisine is popular among the Lebanese clientele and, whilst by no means bad, is almost beside the point. Go to Asia for the debauched and self-indulgent atmosphere and to party among its crowd of beautiful people. Book in advance, dress up and make a night of it.

Food 7, Service 8, Atmosphere 9

Aziz, Kantari, Hamra
Tel: 01 358 000
Open: 7pm–1am daily $35

French, high-class and located slightly off the beaten track, Aziz is without doubt one of the best restaurants in town. Despite its unpromising location on the first floor of a nondescript building on a main through road, Aziz serves up a *smorgasbord* of rich and

delicious treats – from snails to incredible steaks and exquisite desserts. The wine list, which is vast and expensive, is one of the best in town, and the décor simple and elegant, with light flooding in from the vast windows all along one side. After 50 years in the business it's not surprising the place has a regular following (although it's unlikely that any vegetarians feature among them). Once you've experienced the food and attentive service you'll understand why Aziz is one Beirut restaurant not to be missed. A perfect spot for romantic dinners. For those wanting to take the taste of Aziz away, there is also a delicatessen on the ground floor.

Food 9, Service 9, Atmosphere 8

Al Balad, Ahdab Street, Downtown
Tel: 01 985 375
Open: midday–1am daily $15

Possibly the best cheap Lebanese restaurant downtown, Al Balad is an absolute delight whether you choose to dine alfresco or inside. Small, it can accommodate only 30 diners inside and another 30 on the terrace, but it is comfortable, with attentive service. The menu is a typical mix of home-cooked Lebanese *mezze* to start with and grills – chicken and lamb kebabs – to follow, with a surprisingly complete wine list. Al Balad stands out because of its service, the quality of its food and most of all its

value for money. In the busy central area just off Place de l'Etoile, it is the perfect restaurant to enjoy a relaxing meal without feeling suffocated by the hordes of tourists.

Food 9, Service 8, Atmosphere 8

Balthus, Minaa El Hosn, Ghandour Building, Downtown
Tel: 01 371 177
Open: 1–3.30pm, 8:30–11.30pm daily $40

Balthus is one of Beirut's best known French brasseries. Its beige and brown décor, with simple wooden tables and chairs, plays host to a rather grand crowd. At lunchtime in particular, Balthus is the haunt of businessmen, politicians and bankers who descend from the Grand Serail – Beirut's equivalent of Whitehall. The menu is typical brasserie fare and limited as such, but what it lacks in choice it makes up for in quality. Particularly impressive are the foïe gras and the lamb gigot with gratin dauphinois. As with all high-end eateries in Beirut the wine list is extensive,

with a comprehensive selection of French and local wines (which are more reasonable and often delicious). Balthus is a good safe bet, but be aware that service can be a little terse and the atmosphere relatively staid.

Food 8, Service 5, Atmosphere 7

The Beirut Cellar, Tabaris, Achrafieh
Tel: 01 216 990
Open: 11am–1am daily $30

A veteran restaurant with almost 30 years of active service, The Beirut Cellar is located in a quiet area of Achrafieh in between Monnot Street and Gemayzeh. Popular with an older, elegant crowd who look nostalgically back to the days of the civil war, it was one of the few functioning restaurants during that period. Designed like a Swiss chalet, with wooden beams and white plaster walls, it has recently been taken over by an old Beiruti family and revamped with mirrors and modern designer lighting, a mix of high tables, bar stool chairs and low tables, all in red, and a covered outdoor terrace. The French–Italian menu offers a rather predictable array of salads, pastas and steaks, while the wine list includes decent local and French vintages. Being an old favourite, the Cellar gets packed – so remember to book ahead.

Food 6/7, Service 8, Atmosphere 7

The Blue Elephant, Searock Hotel, Raouche
Tel: 01 788 588
Open: 7pm–2am daily $20

In a town obsessed with international cuisine there's a plethora of restaurants to choose from; however, Thai restaurant The Blue

Elephant remains a perennial favourite for a night out. Although not particularly chic, it has a vibe all of its own and the location, next to the Corniche with views over the Mediterranean, makes a pleasant change from Gemayzeh and Monnot Street. The décor is a trifle tacky – think waterfalls and giant goldfish, enlivened during August by Thai folk dancers – but it is actually fantastically relaxing. The food is typical Thai – chicken satay, tom yam prawn soup and a fine emerald chicken, for example – and the drinks plentiful and simple. All in all, a fun and relaxed place to come, and great for a stroll by the sea afterwards to aid the digestion.

Food 8, Service 7, Atmosphere 8

Brookes, Rue Gouraud, Gemayzeh
Tel: 01 570 807
Open: 11am–12.30am. Closed Mondays. $15

Brookes is a relatively recent addition to Gemayzeh's burgeoning dining scene and is the brainchild of British ex-pat Mark Cornwall. Simply decorated, with a heavy, dark wooden bar and tables set off by plain walls with rusted mirrors, and a blackboard menu in one corner, it has the look and feel of a gastropub – a relative rarity in Beirut. And the food is typical British gastro-pub fare: fried Camembert with cranberry sauce and beer-battered fish and chips, all of it good and tasty. Brookes is perfect for a quiet evening meal or for a relaxing Sunday brunch, with a wine list that includes Lebanese and French, and even an expensively out of place Chateau Latour. The owner has lived in Beirut for over a decade so he knows what works on the scene. With low lighting and funky jazz, Brookes is ideal for just chilling and eating, encouraging a seriously relaxed and cool crowd to return day after day.

Food 8, Service 8, Atmosphere 8/9

● **Casablanca, Ain el Mreisseh, Manara**
Tel: 01 369 334
Open: 11am–1am. Closed Mondays. $30

Casablanca is one of Beirut's most famous restaurants. An atmospheric place in a traditional French Mandate period Lebanese house by the sea, Casablanca is perfect for Sunday brunch, lunch or dinner. It's run by Beirut's legendary Johnny Farah and his Asian wife, who concentrate on the style and quality of (unsurprisingly) East-meets-West fusion food. The daily menu includes good, fresh fish and fantastic lobster served with organic vegetables brought in from the Farahs' farm in the countryside. Over the years a devoted clientele has kept it lively and filled with people, making booking a necessity any day of the week. On the down-side the acoustics are poor and it can get noisy, especially when there's a DJ installed (Thursday to Sunday).

Food 8, Service 8, Atmosphere 8

Centrale, Mar Maroun Street, Saifi/Gemyazeh
Tel: 01 575 858
Open: 7pm–3am daily $45

Tucked away on a side street just across from the artsy quarter
of Beirut's Saifi Village, Centrale is distinct for its design, food and
– for this location – longevity (it's reached the grand old age of
three). It's a little hard to find – look out for the tree-lined alleyway with a double line of red lights leading to the restaurant. The
brainwave of Beiruti architect Bernard Khoury, the man who built
the legendary BO18 nightclub (see Party), Centrale is a super-
modern open-plan space with high ceilings, but inside a traditional
house. In the summer you can eat outside in the delightful

covered courtyard that feels like the garden of an Italian villa. The food is a French fusion mix served by accommodating staff to a soundtrack of hip lounge music. A trip to Centrale is a worthwhile (if expensive) experience, particularly for the atmosphere and lashings of exquisite taste, and look out for the Lebanese wines on offer. Arrive a little early or stay a little late and ride the elevator up to the stunning rooftop bar for a pre- or post- parandial cocktail.

Food 9, Service 8, Atmosphere 10

Le Chef, Gouraud Street, Gemayzeh
Tel: 01 445 373
Open: 10am–10 pm daily $10

Le Chef is something of an institution in Beirut. Located next to the picturesque Saint Nicholas steps, and run by jack-of-all-trades maître d' Charbel (he'll find you anything from an apartment for rent to a car for sale), Le Chef offers tasty, good-value Lebanese fare in a relaxed and very Lebanese atmosphere. The open kitchen and low-grade mural on one of the otherwise white walls hardly make for the most salubrious of dining experiences, but it remains enduringly popular. Most Beirut residents who are in the know swear by it and Le Chef is always full with the unlikeliest of characters.

Food 8, Service 6, Atmosphere 8

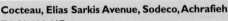

Cocteau, Elias Sarkis Avenue, Sodeco, Achrafieh

Tel: 01 616 617
Open: 8pm–1am daily $35

This upmarket restaurant serving decent French food is named after avant-garde French writer, poet and film-maker Jean Cocteau, a frequent visitor to Lebanon, and specifically the ruins of Baalbek, which he adored. The décor is a melange of subtle beiges and creams with touches of extravagance, notably bottles of champagne dressed by Jean Paul Gaultier in red rubber corsets, and Cocteau-bilia, including a portrait of the man himself above the bar complete with lines of his poetry. The lampshades on the ceiling are made to look like a bookshelf stacked with Cocteau's works. A relatively affluent clientele populate the refectory-style tables, which can be fun if you're in the mood to get to know your neighbours, but not the sort of place for a night of whispered romance.

Food 7, Service 8, Atmosphere 6

Al Dente, Abdel Wahab el Inglizi Street, Achrafieh

Tel: 01 202 440
Open: midday–3pm, 7pm–1am daily $38

Located in this popular Achrafieh street dotted with galleries and boutique fashion stores, Al Dente is an Italian eaterie in a traditional Lebanese house. Full of local character and popular among the fashionable older crowd, including a few politicians who you're likely to find dining discreetly in the corners, Al Dente has been around for almost a decade, quite an accomplishment in Beirut. Serving great home-made pasta and fine risottos, complemented by a decent international wine list, Al Dente is calm and collected, with top-notch service. Worth reserving to avoid disappointment.

Food 8, Service 7, Atmosphere 7

Diwan Sultan Ibrahim, Minet el Hosn, Downtown
Tel: 01 989 989   www.sultanbrahim.com
Open: midday–2pm, 7pm–midnight daily $20

One of downtown's best seafood and Lebanese restaurants, Diwan is a laid-back spot tucked away from the main drag, and a

great pit-stop if you've been walking the streets. Go for fish fresh from the Med, notably sea bass, *mallifa*, red mullet and *bizri* (deep-fried small sardines, a local speciality) as well as traditional Lebanese grilled dishes and *mezze*. Housed in a relatively new building, Diwan's design is rather formal and straightforward, but the service is strong and there are tables outside. Well-priced fresh fish in central Beirut and well worth a visit.

> **Food 9, Service 8, Atmosphere 7**

Eau de Vie, Intercontinental Phoenicia Hotel, Ain El Mreisseh, Downtown
Tel: 01 369 100
Open: midday–2.30pm, 9pm–1am daily $40

Eau de Vie is one of those restaurants you would love to be able to hate but you just simply can't. It is pure high life: a potent mixture of Mediterranean views, exquisite surroundings and gourmet food. Located on the top floor of the Phoenicia Hotel, the atmosphere is intimate and relaxed – think well-spaced tables,

leather armchairs, soft carpeting, low lighting and dark wooden cabinets stocked with wine and cigars. The clientele, as you might expect, is affluent, chic and stylish. If it all sounds a little extravagant, it is, but the food, service and views make it really special. Hotel restaurants can be a little staid, but at Eau de Vie you soon forget where you are as you stare out over the bay, with a piano softly played in the background. The menu is impressive, the food an enticing mix of delicately prepared dishes and fantastically fresh seafood.

Food 9, Service 8, Atmosphere 9

Fennel, Rue Clemenceau, Hamra
Tel: 01 211 400
Open: 11am–midnight. Closed Mondays. $25

Located in the Weavers Building in Clemenceau, on the site of the former News Café, Fennel has quietly established itself among Beirut's food-loving population as something of a home-from-home. Spread over two floors, the all-white interior looks out through wide glass windows onto a plant-filled terrace and the hulkingly ramshackle old Holiday Inn. Owner and recipe designer Ahmed Husseini describes the food simply as 'Italian cuisine in an unclassical style' – or, roughly translated, experimental Italian. 'My philosophy is: have quality on your side, rely on the freshest and best ingredients, and let talented staff experiment with the recipes,' Husseini says. 'The result is all in the taste.' The pasta is, of course, made fresh daily on site and is close to perfection coupled with a bottle of Castigliono Chianti. With its wide selection of international magazines and papers to pore over, Fennel is a perfect place for Sunday brunch.

Food 8, Service 7, Atmosphere 8

India, Maarad Street, Downtown
Tel: 01 987 737
Open: 7pm–midnight daily $25

There are about five Indian restaurants in Beirut but India stands
out for the strength of its food and its atmosphere. The dark and
colonial décor is supposed to evoke the feeling of ancient India,
but although it's slightly off-target it has nevertheless created a
comfortable downtown experience where guests lounge at tables
or perch, cocktail in hand, at the bar. The men behind it – Serge
Chehab, Raji Varma and Anthony Baladi – really understand the
essence of Punjabi cuisine, preparing delicately spiced curries for
any taste. There's a good selection of grilled or curried vegetarian
dishes as well as delicious lamb and seafood dishes, and undoubtedly the best *biriani* and *popadoms* you'll find in the Middle East.
India is a relaxing retreat away from the cafés of Downtown,
which endlessly spill their *narguileh*-smoking clientele on to the
pavements.

Food 8, Service 7, Atmosphere 8

Julia's, Abdel Wahab el Inglizi Street, Achrafieh
Tel: 01 219 539
Open: 1–4pm, 9pm–midnight daily $30

Located in the heart of plush Achrafieh, on one of the most

exclusive streets, Julia's is an exquisite blend of the modern and the traditional. It is housed in a traditional French Mandate period stone building, whose cracked, faded walls and large windows create a comfortable atmosphere. An international fusion menu betrays more than a touch of French influence; consequently the meat is cooked to perfection and the sauces are almost sensuous. The wine list draws from Lebanese Kefraya and Ksaara reds and whites to a cool Sancerre as well as some more extravagantly indulgent options. Unsurprisingly, the local chef learned his trade in France and the service is spot on. A modern zinc bar is ideal if you just want to drink, which makes Julia's a good spot for a romantic nightcap. Booking in advance is a must.

Food 9, Service 8, Atmosphere 8

Karam Beirut, Bazerkan Street, Downtown
Tel: 01 991 222
Open: midday–midnight daily. $25

One of the better downtown Lebanese restaurants, Karam Beirut is built over two floors and looks onto a tree-lined square with an attractive mosque on the far side. Although a plethora of tourists rather dilutes the atmosphere, its quiet position away from Maarad Street and Place de l'Etoile, minimal décor and delicious food are more than enough justification for a visit. The luxuriant Lebanese fare includes amazing grilled *kebbe* balls, lamb *kafta*, *hummus* and aubergine dips with pine seeds and amazing local olives and flat bread served along with good *arak* to aid digestion and divine Lebanese sweets (especially the *baclawa*). The maître d' can be a bit grumpy but overall Karam wins the prize for best local cuisine in the downtown area.

Food 9, Service 7, Atmosphere 7

Mandarine, Rachid Karame Street, Verdun
Tel: 01 781 000
Open: 7pm–midnight daily $25

Mandarine is one of Beirut's oldest restaurants, simply decorated and now appealing to the ladies-who-lunch, weary from taxing shopping trips to the boutiques of trendy Verdun. Lebanese and

fusion cuisine are the order of the day in this small but relaxed environment. It's rather quiet, and its location is not the most happening in town, but it does benefit from an innovative conveyor belt for Arabic *mezze*, a concept so obviously lifted from Lebanon's sushi bars. Look out for the *foul modama*, fried cauliflower in tahini and the *manoushie*.

Food 8, Service 7, Atmosphere 8

Mayass, Trabaud Street, Achrafieh
Tel: 01 215 046
Open: 7pm–1am daily $20

Mayass has rightfully earned its reputation for excellent food at reasonable prices. This traditional Armenian–Lebanese eaterie serves fantastic *mezze* and Armenian specialities from Aleppo, in a cosy atmosphere more reminiscent of a Mediterranean island than an old Achrafieh house. Try the fantastic Armenian specialities of *manti* (dumplings), *beurak* (filo cheese and parsley fingers), *soujouk* (sausages sautéed in tomato) and *basterma* (beef pastrami), and the best dish on the menu, the magical *kafta* (grilled lamb with spices) in a hot, fresh cherry sauce. Add to this good value for money, wonderful atmosphere, romantic live entertainment (an old Armenian who table-hops armed with a three-string guitar to serenade you with any song of your choice – from Shakira to Sinatra to Fairuz – in a beautiful falsetto), and

you have the ingredients for a truly special evening. Booking a couple of days in advance is always necessary.

Food 9, Service 9, Atmosphere 9

Mayrig, 282 Pasteur Street, Gemayzeh
Tel: 01 572 121
Open: midday–11.30pm daily $25

One of the best Armenian–Lebanese restaurants in town, Mayrig is symbolic of the melting-pot of cultures that includes Beirut. Situated in an old house in the popular Gemayzeh quarter of town, it has walls of ancient stone, floors thick with Persian carpets and a warm and welcoming atmosphere. Diners range from Arab tourists to local intellectuals, students and trendy pre-clubbers. If you like Lebanese food and are feeling adventurous try the *kebbe naihe* (raw ground meat with couscous and spices eaten with bread), followed by the traditional Armenian dishes of *havgitov basterma* (spicy sausage on toasted bread topped with a fried quail's egg). The desserts are always worth leaving room for, and, be warned, do tend to be incredibly rich. Mayrig is perfect for couples, but you'll definitely need to lie down afterwards. Not to be missed.

Food 9, Service 7, Atmosphere 7

Memoires de Chine, El Maliye Street, Downtown
Tel: 01 996 633
Open: midday–1am daily $20

Arguably the best Chinese restaurant in Beirut (although the competition is thin on the ground), Memoires de Chine offers stylish décor and comfortable seating as well as good, but not necessarily adventurous, food. The mood is romantic, with lighting kept low throughout lunch and dinner – perfect for illicit (and indeed perfectly licit) liaisons. All the food is pretty good, but the numerous duck dishes are the restaurant's speciality. The wine list is admirable and includes a solid Lebanese selection, served to a high-class clientele (although note that it can be extremely touristy during the high-season summer months). If you're craving a Chinese, then Memoires de Chine is your place.

Food 7, Service 8, Atmosphere 7

Al Mijana, Abdel Wahab el Inglizi, Achrafieh
Tel: 01 328 082
Open: midday–3pm, 8pm–midnight. Closed Saturdays. $30

Mijana is a traditional Lebanese restaurant in a beautifully restored Ottoman building, furnished with opulent, comfortable chairs and infused with more than a hint of the Orient. You can eat indoors or outdoors in the covered courtyard. The menu features traditional Lebanese specialities alongside the ubiquitous mezze – the red *hummus* and deep fried potatoes are particularly good, as is the *shish taouk* chicken doused in lashings of garlic. It's reasonably priced and the service is second to none, although nothing less would be tolerated by the wealthy crowd Mijana attracts. A high end Beirut restaurant, perfect for a leisurely meal watching the glamour-safari of fantastically bejewelled ladies and cigar-puffing men trading gossip.

Food 8, Service 9, Atmosphere 8

L'O, Gouraud Street, Gemayzeh
Tel: 01 560 480
Open: midday–4pm, 7pm–1am daily $30

This exclusive fusion restaurant is the latest offering from the veteran Beirut restaurateurs who ran (the incredibly trendy but now closed) Food Yard and Otium. L'O, standing for original, is sandwiched between the more downbeat cafés and bars of Gemayzeh. Original it is – from its futuristic *Star Wars* shuttle design, reminiscent of Damien Hirst's now-defunct Pharmacy in Notting Hill, to the ever-changing light display on the ceiling. A deliciously varied menu, from the sashimi toast and *chorizo* vinaigrette salad, is served alongside a DJ playing lounge sounds. The service is oddly lazy for a such a reputable place, but this doesn't seem to dent its popularity. Lunchtimes are crowded with businessmen and ladies-who-lunch while dinner attracts a more mixed crowd of young creatives. L'O gets top marks for style, music and atmosphere, and the food's good too.

Food 8, Service 6, Atmosphere 9

Olive, Abdel Wahab el Inglizi Street, Achrafieh
Tel: 01 211 711
Open: 1pm–11pm daily $20

Olive opened at the end of 2004 in the ground floor of a French Mandate period apartment building in this exclusive Achrafieh street. Low-key in style it provides a refreshing change from some of the more high-end joints nearby. Run by a Lebanese

mother and son team, it's fully vegetarian, serving a strictly organic menu of hot and cold dishes and salads – the infectious Kimo will explain to you the benefits and delights of organic vegetarian food with a ready smile. The décor is simple, light and airy, and the tiled floors and wooden tables give you the feeling that you are still in the living room of an old house. But without doubt the main delights of eating here are the fresh organic juices – try the ginger and carrot juice – and the fresh baked cakes. Organic deli food is on sale, too; but if meat's not your thing, or if you're just in need of a detox after Beirut's exhausting nightlife, you'll love this place.

Food 8, Service 8, Atmosphere 9

People Brasserie, Aishti, Saad Zarghoul St, Downtown
Tel: 01 974 444
Open: 12.30–4pm, 7–10pm daily $40

People is one of our favourite restaurants in downtown Beirut. Located high on top of Aishti (Beirut's equivalent of Harvey Nichols), People is a relaxed place, with comfortable Driade chairs in transparent Plexiglas, a long oak table and designer Italian sofas. You can just go for a drink or coffee but it's more than likely you'll be tempted by the menu as chef Franck Paulmier's brasserie-style food hits the spot. People draws in a uniformly affluent crowd of all ages but with a common love of food. A good downtown alternative to the numerous street-side

cafés and restaurants, it's perfect for lunch or an early dinner (note that it closes with the main store at 10pm).

Food 8, Service 8, Atmosphere 9

La Plage, Ain El Mreisseh, Downtown
Tel: 01 366 222
Open: midday–4pm, 8pm–1am daily $25

La Plage is a little bit special in Beirut's line-up of restaurants, and a favourite among the locals, eschewing elegance and sophistication for a vibrant atmosphere, fantastic food and friendly staff. It's located on the seafront at the eastern end of the Corniche, and you can dine inside or out with the Mediterranean as a beautiful backdrop. A primarily pescian menu – the Sultan Brahim is good to start and the Loukous sea bass drenched in lemon butter sauce is otherworldly – includes a few salads, *mezze* and burgers for the landlubbers. The wine list is decent, comprising mostly French and Italian, but Lebanese wines, especially the Ksara and Kefraya, go well with fish. It's well worth coming for a summer lunch, if only for the walk past the swimming pool where numerous sun worshippers preen themselves mercilessly – making for great dining entertainment.

Food 9, Service 9, Atmosphere 8

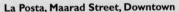

La Posta, Maarad Street, Downtown
Tel: 01 970 597 www.loaposta-beirut.com
Open: midday–1am daily $30

One of the most popular Italian restaurants in downtown Beirut,
La Posta gets as full as its menu – which offers a total of 48 main
courses and a 50-strong wine list. It's an eclectically designed
place with the plum seats at the back, where you can avoid the
noise from bustling Maarad Street and enjoy the most fantastic
view of towering columns from the city's Roman ruins. The food
is typically Italian and the portions generous, featuring a good
selection of risottos and fish alongside pizzas and pastas. We
recommend leaving room for pudding as La Posta does a mean
ice cream – try the pear sorbet with grappa.

Food 8, Service 8, Atmosphere 8

Au Premier, Intercontinental Vendome Hotel, Ain El Mreisseh, Downtown
Tel: 01 368 300
Open: midday–2.30pm, 9pm–1am. Closed Sundays. $35

Located on the first floor of the Intercontinental Le Vendôme
Hotel, Au Premier excels at pure French gastronomy. To ring the
changes, each month the restaurant features a top Michelin guest
chef serving up five-star cuisine – Alain Reix from the Jules Verne

restaurant at the Eiffel Tower in Paris is just one of the many. Decorated like a Parisian apartment, its unique spaces range from a dining room stuffed with antique *objets* and original paintings, to a library and a garden room. This is a rich place with rich food that really lives up to its billing – and its prices. From the exquisite *foie gras* starters to a perfect *filet de boeuf* and melt-in-your-mouth *crème brûlée*, with a wine list to compliment, Au Premier is undoubtedly one of Beirut's top culinary spots. The hotel atmosphere can be slightly quiet but at the end of the day it is all about the food.

Food 9, Service 8, Atmosphere 8

Relais de l'Entrecôte, Abdel Wahab el Inglezi, Achrafieh
Tel: 01 332 088
Open: midday–3pm, 7pm–midnight daily $25

A little bit of Paris on the corner of Monnot Street and Abdel Wahab el Inglizi Street, Relais is a perfect *steak frîtes* restaurant complete with curtained windows, wood interior and polite service. There is no menu as such, just the question of how do you like your entrecôte cooked and what you would like to drink with it. Relais is one of those restaurants that has lasted in Beirut because it simply is what it is, you know what you are getting and you know it is going to be good. The puddings are also exceptional, especially the chocolate fondant and the profiteroles. It's good if visiting on your own or with friends, as the atmosphere is always loud and vibrant, with a Lebanese crowd taken from every walk of life. Sundays are particularly full. Vegetarians be warned there is nothing for you here.

Food 8, Service 8, Atmosphere 9

Salmontini, Ahdab Street, Downtown
Tel: 01 990 777   www.lamaisondusaumon.com
Open: 11am–midnight daily $40

Subtitled 'The House of Salmon', Salmontini is a place for fans of the big pink fish, and here they cook it in any one of a thousand different ways. Salmontini is a large restaurant in Beirut's downtown, decorated like the dining hall of cruise ship and you end

up feeling like the captain in the haughty, but somewhat kitsch, surroundings bedecked with paintings, mirrors, wood panels and intimate booths. The salmon is shipped in fresh from Scotland and then transformed into both classic and creative dishes – try the salmon with *wasabi* and basil, or the more Lebanese-style grilled salmon with couscous and *harissa*. Salmontini attracts Beirut's affluent business crowd (and has prices to match), but it is delicious, decadent and typically downtown.

Food 9, Service 8, Atmosphere 7

Scallywags, St Joseph University Street, Achrafieh
Tel: 03 046 289
Open: 7pm–1am daily $15

This is one of the cosiest and most colourful little eateries in town; the man behind it is the London-based Richard Defontaine who came to Beirut on holiday and loved it enough to open a place here – you'll often find him getting up and doing a little live karaoke for his guests when he is in town. Scallywags is small, with about four tables seating only 20 or so, and a homely kitchen in full view of the customers – so homely, in fact, that you can always join in if you feel so inclined. Fusion cuisine is the order of the day – Italian, French and English cooked in Far Eastern spices, all of which is tasty and comforting. There is a menu but half the time Defontaine just serves up whatever he

feels like cooking on the day. Fun, friendly and hugely popular.

Food 8, Service 7, Atmosphere 8

Solea, Monnot Street, Achrafieh
Tel: 01 330 119
Open: 7pm–1am daily $20

Midway down Monnot Street lies Solea, the only authentic Spanish restaurant in Beirut. Run by the beautiful Zeina, Solea not only has exquisite *tapas* and thirst-quenching sangria but also live flamenco music on Wednesdays and Saturdays. Nestled between a couple of bars and recognizable by the pure gypsy red curtain hanging over the door, the space is designed like an Andalusian cave and is wonderfully intimate. Try the *albondegas* and the *chorizo*, and the *paella* is particularly good. The waiters can be a bit dopey and, when busy – which is most nights – the food takes a while to get to the table, but when it arrives it is well worth the wait. The atmosphere is infectious and you can't help but tap along with the *guitarista*. Outside, and a real selling point, is the intimate tropical garden complete with the Solea's resident cats. There's little to beat relaxed Spanish dining on a summer's night.

Food 9, Service 7, Atmosphere 9

Sushi Bar, Abdel Wahab el Inglizi Street, Achrafieh
Tel: 01 338 555
Open: midday–midnight daily $25

The best of Beirut's numerous sushi bars gets top marks not just for the standard of its food but also its freshness and cleanliness. Appealing to serious diners, the interior features rice-paper panels on the ceiling, a dominant central bar surrounded by tall tables and chairs, pine wood walls and comfy low running sofas where patrons can sit and relax with a glass of champagne. The extensive menu has the usual *maki*, sashimi and sushi but try the Spicy Fever *maki* or the special sashimi, with large portions of fish on ice and fabulous scallops marinated in sweet vinegar sauce. Definitely aimed at an upmarket crowd, Sushi Bar is suitably expensive but worth it.

Food 8, Service 8, Atmosphere 7

La Tabkha, Rue Gouraud, Gemayzeh
Tel: 01 579 000
Open: 11am–4pm. Closed Sundays. $10

A new Lebanese restaurant and one of the most innovative in Beirut, where Grandma's home cooking is served up Nobu-fashion in a stylish space designed for comfort. The concept is Lebanese fast food, according to its general manager Fady Saba, the man who opened legendary Beirut bar/club Zinc over seven years ago (see Drink). With its wide glass windows and comfortable seating up against wood tables, Tabkha is always packed and the atmosphere always buzzing. You'll hear the usual patois of French, Arabic and English spoken by the trendy Gemayzeh artist crowd who mix in here with the local advertising and banking execs. There are three daily specials available and a traditional Lebanese *mezze* buffet. The walls are decorated with works by local artists and photographers.

Food 7, Service 8, Atmosphere 7

Tamaris, Patchi Building, Weygand Street, Downtown
Tel: 01 996 500 www.tamaris-restaurant.com
Open: midday–midnight daily $15

Michelin three-starred chef Alain Ducasse is the man behind Tamaris, an exclusive downtown restaurant specializing in desserts. Named and themed after a Mediterranean tree, from the pink napkins and menus to the brown cocoa plates, Tamaris is planted on the top floor of the Paatchi building in the exclusive downtown shopping area, and it made us feel rich. That said, Tamaris is not particularly expensive, it just concentrates on what it does best: typical French patisserie delicacies such as macaroons, *mille feuille* and éclairs. Mixing French and Mediterranean influences, Ducasse offers a range of little dishes along the lines of *tartine* with tuna in oil, artichoke and sun-dried tomatoes. An older crowd fills the well-designed and harmonious space, especially in the afternoon when weary shoppers from nearby boutiques feel they have deserved a well-earned rest. Tamaris is really about lunch rather than dinner but is great for a diet-busting treat at any time.

Food 8, Service 8, Atmosphere 7

Wadi Walima, Makdisi Street, Hamra
Tel: 01 745 933
Open: midday–3pm, 8pm–midnight daily $10

Tucked away in the once-cosmopolitan and resolutely commer-cial Hamra, this wonderful little restaurant, with its beautiful gar-den terrace, provides an unexpected oasis of calm in the city. An old house with little rooms leading off from the centre, it is sim-

ply decorated and offers a creative Lebanese menu with local wine and a delicious brunch option. Better for lunch than dinner, Wadi Walima never gets too crowded and is well worth a visit if you're in Hamra. This is a truly local hangout with good service and good food at reasonable prices.

Food 7, Service 7, Atmosphere 7

Yabani, Damascus Road, Achrafieh
Tel: 01 211 113
Open: 8pm–1am daily $25

The fashionable Yabani, another Bernard Khoury designed restaurant, can be found parallel to Monnot Street and close to its bars and clubs, but you won't readily see it because it's underground. A circular Japanese restaurant, Yabani is designed around its massive central lift shaft and has skylights that look up to street level above, making it surprisingly bright. We liked the booths located in a crescent around the central sushi bar that wraps around the lift shaft, but it does get loud as sound from surrounding speakers travels easily around the space. The food is straightforward sushi and sashimi, mixed in with some more inventive creations and good *ceviche* dishes, all served with great attention to detail by Philippino staff dressed in traditional Japanese outfits. Reservations essential.

Food 8, Service 9, Atmosphere 9

Hg2 Beirut

drink...

If there is any pastime more prevalent than drinking in Beirut, then we can't find it. This is not to paint Beirutis as a bunch of alcoholics – far from it in fact – as many people do not drink at all, especially those who take their religion seriously. But ultimately, as in other Mediterranean countries such as Spain and Italy, drinking is a way of life, and when you buy a drink you get a drink, there are no small measures of alcohol here. Your glass is filled to the top and you can get remarkably tipsy without breaking the bank. Beirut is not your typical Arab capital and in many ways, especially in the central areas, it is thoroughly Westernized. Beirut differs from many Middle Eastern countries in that there is no stigma attached to drinking, and most of the town's bars do a bustling business.

Beirut is a party town and the bar culture reflects that. Places range from small pubs with little in the way of design (Hole In The Wall, Celtic, 37 Degrees) to the more sophisticated but small bars with continually lively atmospheres (Dragonfly, Torino Express), which are filled nightly with local Beirutis out to have fun.

Then there are the designer bars attracting a more dressed-up and stylish crowd of 20- and 30-somethings who want to party and really sample the barman's creative cocktail skills. These places (Centrale, Sky Bar, Shah Lounge, Baby M, Bar Med) are often well planned out, with exquisite interior design and pumping sound systems, luring in a crowd who want to dance. They only differ from nightclubs in that there is no central dance-floor, which means you dance where you can: the bar, the table and the chairs are all fair game. Which means things can get pretty hot and sweaty.

The highest concentration of the best bars is in Achrafieh by way of the famous Monnot Street and Gemayzeh. Others can be found in Hamra and the rebuilt downtown area.

Nearly all the bars serve some sort of finger food and some, such as Pacifico and Lila Braun, offer a full menu, so you'll never find yourself having to search for a late night kebab (although the option is always there).

Musically Beirut bars offer a wonderfully eclectic mix. Some have DJs because it just wouldn't do not to; these generally play a commercial mix of hip-hop. R&B, funk, electronica and nu-wave. The best places for cutting-edge music are Club Social, Lila Braun and Torino Express, while Art Lounge often puts on specialist nights. More low-key and attractive bars such as Barometre play a selection of traditional Arabic music.

The bar scene in Beirut is incredibly popular and sometimes excruciatingly trendy. Most people don't think twice about dressing up to go out – the culture is very much about being seen. Don't be intimidated by Lebanese women – most are phenomenally beautiful and do dress to impress. The men are friendly and it is not difficult to end up deep in conversation, but it's best to steer clear of religion and war, always sensitive subjects in a city with so many different sects. If you do open that door, be prepared for debate. Some bars have a door policy, but not all, and unless you are falling over or in a group of 10 guys, you should be allowed in.

The best bars for music and a bit of dancing are Club Social and Lila Braun; for chilling and conversation, Dragonfly and Barometre; and for sports and beer, Hole In The Wall and Celtic. The one down-side of the bar culture is the fact that many people don't think twice about drinking and driving, so be careful about accepting rides and look out if you're walking back to your hotel. Taxis are widely available.

Of all the little bars in the alleyway off the Monnot Street, 37 Degrees has the most charm. The bar staff are friendly and the high tables and chairs which spill out onto a terrace area in the summer perfect for people-watching – and the crowd around here is certainly worth watching. Striking up conversations with the many English speakers you'll find here is relatively easy, so 37 Degrees makes a good starting-point for a night out, especially if you want to meet people and pick their brains. Generous measures of spirits and some decent cocktails will ensure that the night starts off with a bang.

1975, Monnot Street, Achrafieh
Tel: 03 323 700
Open: 8pm–2am daily

1975 almost didn't get a mention because of the polarized opinions that local Beirutis have of the place. Located in the popular party street next to the designer haunts, this bar, on two levels, is themed on the Lebanese civil war. The walls are decorated with bullet holes and propped up with sandbags, while old Lebanese bank notes hang from the walls. Two bars on different levels help muffle the somewhat patriotic singing of the crowd, who after a certain amount crank up the volume and churn out hits from local legend Fairuz and old nationalistic anthems. A sophisticated scene this isn't – seating is basic and the drinks are straightforward – but you do feel like you're an intrepid reporter holed up in a bunker in this former war zone. 1975 is worth a visit to check out the extraordinary Lebanese bar scene, and fun to experience.

Art Lounge, River Bridge, Karantina
Tel: 03 997 676
Open: 6pm–2am daily

Located in a warehouse-style space in a former cotton factory under the Karantina Bridge, this is the city's only laid-bar and gallery space in one. It's an intriguing visual space full of retro furniture, where works of Pop Art dot the walls in vast swathes

of colour, complemented by random sculptures and everyday objects such as brooms and glasses. Every weekend the space, which feels rather like a New York artist's chill-out open house, features local and international DJs spinning everything from breakbeats to deep funk. A very off-the-cuff bar lurks at the back of the room, keeping everyone well lubricated and in high spirits. Owner ad exec Nino Azzi encourages a relaxed crowd; there's no door policy, so you get a mixture of Beirut's wannabe Bohemians and suited advertising types.

Baby M, El Maliye Street, Downtown
Tel: 01 992 993
Open: 9pm–3am daily

One of downtown's livelier bars, located underground in a street close to the parliament building, Baby M (Baby Mandaloun) is the younger brother of Mandouloun, one of the bigger Arabic night-clubs in town, located on the Damascus Road. Large and L-shaped, the long bar follows the contours of the room. On every side large plush couches and tables are filled with good-looking 20-something locals. In one corner a DJ spins predominantly commercial R&B and Arabic *chaabi* pop to get the crowd in the mood. The bouncers can be difficult and the way to ensure entry is to book a table in advance; doing so requires you to buy at least one bottle of liquor for about $100. But don't worry; if you look good and are in a mixed group you should have no prob-lems. Once inside, Baby M will have you dancing on the tables.

Bar Med, Monnot Street, Achrafieh
Tel: 01 219 525
Open: 10pm–4am daily

Bar Med opened in the summer of 2004 and after a year is still open, which for Monnot Street is pretty good going. This bar/club is all velvets and red sofas and silver walls, and worth a visit if you can make it through the door. Looking too much like a tourist will get you nowhere, but act casual and dress with a bit of class and in you go. The music is mainly house with a little Arabic thrown in from the likes of DJ Romax hailing from Amsterdam, while on specialist nights it becomes an '80s school disco throwback. The bar is a *Cheers*-style creation in the centre of the space with customers milling around it. One of the places to hit late in the evening, it's got plenty of space for dancing – and in Bar Med, more often than not, the girls get up on the bar and get down.

Barometre, Makhoul Street, Hamra
Tel: 01 367 229
Open: 7pm–2am daily

Barometre is possibly the most Boho hang-out in town. And that means it is full of intellectuals, *oud* players, musicians, writers, hacks and a few students. The tiny room with a small bar and four tables doesn't seem much of a place, but what it has is local charm – and you definitely don't get many tourists walking in. Barometre is more about bottles of beer and straight liquor than fancy cocktails and pink umbrellas. The music is taken from Arabic greats like Umm Khaltoum, Fairuz and Abdel Wahab. Expect great conversations – you can generally include yourself in whatever debate's going on in the corner – and a friendly atmosphere. On special nights, which means whenever the owner feels like it, he'll pick up his *oud* and come and sing some Arabic classical favourites – much to the delight of the locals, who generally sing along loudly and often out of tune.

Biba, Rue Gouraud, Gemayzeh
Tel: 01 474 567
Open: 7pm–1am daily

Biba is a small eccentric bar in Gemayzeh, slightly off the main drag but still well worth a visit. Decorated with the front panels of old pinball machines, as well as large, conical hair-dryers from hair salons resting in front of orange-red walls, Biba is a colourful and eclectic experience, and very much a local hang-out. Appealing to writers and young hipsters, the owner and various DJs play old vinyl and pretty much whatever genre they feel like. Straightforward, no-nonsense drinks are cheap, and are one of Biba's main attractions. A small TV in the corner shows the occasional football or basketball match for local fans. Pop in for an early evening drink or a final tipple before bed.

Celtic, Monnot Street, Achrafieh
Tel: 01 215 933
Open: midday–1am daily

Celtic is one of the few British-style pubs in Beirut today. Serving Caffreys, Heineken and local beer Almaza on tap, it is not surprisingly a popular spot for watching sports – there are four large TVs and a projector screen. Nearly always full, it is located in the new courtyard on Monnot directly on top of Moloko. The interior is fairly plain – a number of high wooden tables and stools seat those not crowded into the bar – and is a great antidote to the town's many overly designed bars. The manager, a man called Berdj, takes great care of any wandering travellers and is happy to point you in the right direction, whether you

want to party, eat or chill. Celtic is a good place to go before a full night of heavy hedonism or to glean some info from the few ex-pat Brits and Westerners who live in Beirut.

Centrale, Saifi Street, Gemayzeh
Tel: 01 575 858
Open: 8pm–3am daily

Perhaps one of the most exquisitely designed bars in town it stands nearly 7 metres in the air in a black steel cylinder reachable only through a 1930s hydraulic lift, a trademark of Centrale's architect, Beirut bad boy Bernard Khoury. The tubular bar is set on top of a converted old Gemayzeh mansion, which houses the equally famous Centrale restaurant below. The bar stretches 10 metres from end to end and about 2 metres wide, so space is at a premium. Weekends can get unbelievably crowded, but it can be wonderfully intimate during the week. Essentially, however, Centrale is a bar one might expect to find in the heart of Manhattan rather than Beirut. The windows behind the bar revolve upwards at the touch of a button to open onto the star-speckled sky at night, a view of Martyr's Square, or the neighbours opposite. Head barman Michel boasts the widest selection of whiskies in town, but they come at a cost. Prepare to break open your wallet here to get down with a deeply funky crowd, young and old, to DJs spinning everything from jazzy house to hard groove to queen Nina Simone herself.

Chez Andre, Hamra Street, Hamra
Tel: 01 740 777
Open: 9pm–2am daily

This little Hamra hole has been a staple in the neighbourhood for many years and is named after its late owner Andre, who famously entertained locals with his brand of spicy humour and good service. Chez Andre is home to an extremely casual crowd, who come for the conversation and the atmosphere in this tiny pub. Much of the intellectual conversation that goes on in Hamra, among professors and students from the American Univeristy of Beirut, or from the bearded chain-smoking writers who have populated Hamra for years, goes on in Chez Andre. Pints are served up to a seriously liquid crowd and fried *halloumi* cheese and bread is on offer to soften the blow. If you can't find Andre's at first, don't worry: it is fairly hidden away inside a covered gallery area of shops just off the street. But stick with it.

Club Social, Saifi Street, Gemayzeh
Tel: 03 333 377
Open: 9pm–3am daily

Club Social attracts one of the hippest crowds in Beirut. An oblong space that used to be a furniture store, with small wood tables stapled to the floor, antique mirrors and lights bought from the Beirut thrift market, it also has constantly changing art displays. Social Club, as its regulars refer to it, is owned by the son of a prominent Baalbeck family, and aims to provide cheap drinks and fantastic music. The no door policy means that the trendy crowd that populates it can come to hear some of the city's best DJs nightly. Sundays are reserved for special events such as Beirut's healthy underground scene, featuring rock and trip-hop bands such as Scrambled Eggs and Soap Kills. More dirty chic than glamour the Social is all about the music, attracting some of Lebanon's finest talents both to drink and play.

District, Damascus Road, Achrafieh
Tel: 03 080 828
Open: 9pm–3am daily

District was built from scratch in 2004, allowing it to create exactly the space it requires. Still relatively fresh on the whole Beirut designer bar scene, it's big and dark, a massive concrete square of a place, with a long bar and numerous low-slung tables. An eclectic mix of loud music graces the top-end sound system, and the crowd of 30-somethings dressed to the nines love it. The DJ, hidden behind a dark mirrored glass screen, occasionally pops his head out but generally leaves everyone to their own devices. The bar, serving delicious daiquiris and ritzy champagne cocktails, has been widened to allow the intoxicated female clientele to gyrate on it seductively later in the evening. District is full of Beirut's most affluent and hedonistically minded citizens – glamour is definitely the order of the day. Dress up, drink up and

abandon all inhibitions.

Dragonfly, Rue Gouraud, Gemayzeh
Tel: 03 664 284
Open: 7pm–2am daily

Abboud is a genius and Abboud tends the bar in Dragonfly, the latest classy drinkerie from Lebanese brothers Michel, Steve and Camille – the clan responsible for the legendary bar Havana in the town of Jounieh, and Pacifico and Lila Braun in Beirut. From Abboud's mango daiquiris and whisky sours to his much sought-after caipirinhas, the man has become a cocktail-making legend in the Lebanese capital and the trio are lucky to have him. Dragonfly sits in a former storage cellar with arched ceilings

next door to Torino Express. Small in size, it is big in personality and attracts a mid-20- to 30-something crowd of trendy, affluent Beirutis, from ad execs to underground musicians. The DJ plays jazz and groove, and occasionally more eclectic drum'n'bass, but the atmosphere buzzes with friendly laughter as locals drink for hours at the marble bar or perched at the high tables opposite.

Hole In the Wall, Monnot Street, Achrafieh
Tel: 03 549 651
Open: 8pm–2am daily

This little bar is exactly what its name suggests. Small, with a couple of high tables, Hole used to be popular with British ex-pats, UN soldiers and heavy pint drinkers – it is one of the few bars that has Caffreys and Heineken on tap – but these days it is the haunt of young Lebanese and students who want to drink à la English pub style. Hole can get crowded, and at weekends the bar has been known to get pretty rowdy. Holding only about 50 people it can get hot, sweaty and noisy, especially with the Hendrix and Led Zeppelin soundtrack blaring from the speakers. As per usual the young and the drunk clamber onto the bar to strut their funky stuff to the Doors or the Rolling Stones. Hole in the Wall is all about drinking, dancing and deep conversation, and is a welcomingly casual affair.

Ice Bar, Monnot Street, Achrafieh
Tel: 01 203 215
Open: 8pm–2am daily

With R&B, rock and hip-hop music, and a couple of live shows every weekend, Ice Bar is much more chilled than most Monnot Street hang-outs. As its name suggests, Ice Bar serves plenty of Smirnoff Ice drinks to a young crowd (the alcopops generation). Oblong in shape and arranged over two floors, it also has a comfortable outside terrace on which to sit and sip an Almaza or L'Aziza (the other local beer). Bar or waitress service makes Ice Bar an easy option, but it's more of an in-and-out place, where you stop for a beer before moving on to another Monnot bar or going out to grab a bite somewhere.

L-Bar, Damascus Road, Achrafieh
Tel: 01 333 833
Open: 9pm–2am daily

L-Bar is popular among an older crowd in Beirut. As you may have guessed it's shaped like an L; ultra-modern in design, the lounge/bar serves good food and plays loud music while the clientele rest against the long bar. Hanging from the ceiling are hundreds of long tubular lights, giving off a calming orange glow, and the plush velvet seats are soft, sleek and easy to sink into. It's all very relaxing, but DJ Ralf Khoury gets the vibe more upbeat later, playing a mix of oriental and house beats. The cocktails are good but not special; however, L-Bar does have all the latest import spirits, which are worth sampling. Generally this is a 30-something place, smart, intimate and less frenetic; if that's not what you want, just pop in for a chilled pre-club vodka.

Leila, El Arz Street, Gemayzeh,
Tel: 03 839 850
Open: 9am–2am daily

A relatively new bar (opened at the end of 2004) that doubles, like Torino Express, as a café by day. A traditional wooden door provides the entrance into what used to be a neighbourhood barbershop, now a small space with simple wood tables and pieces of poetry and art on the walls. Feeling like a library, the bar is set discreetly at the back of the room while a gallery

offers extra seating and a niche for the DJ – who plays a little bit of everything jazz-influenced. The drinks are solid, though not to die for, and the crowd is a mix of alternative and intellectual, making their escape from the main drag of Rue Gouraud. So far Leila is the first bar to open up on Gemayzeh's lower road, but if the continuing gentrification of the street is anything to go by it will soon be joined by many more. Come to Leila for a lunchtime beer, an early drink or as a last stop before bed.

Lila Braun, Monnot Street, Achrafieh
Tel: 01 331 662
Open: 9pm–4am daily

A Shoreditch-style bar with retro furniture and a funky young crowd, Lila Braun is the place to be. Located in the happening Monnot Street in the alleyway that began it all 10 years ago, Lila Braun, named after a 1940s jazz singer, can be reached through a barred gate (and past a bouncer). Serving a fusion cuisine of Thai-oriental food, it is one of the three Beirut stalwarts owned by brothers Camille, Steve and Michel. The cocktails are extremely good (and expensive) – any of the rum numbers will set you up for a night of decadent pleasure. A long bar, with Chesterfield leather sofas for long-limbed models and designer shirts to lounge over, is overlooked by two gallery levels with a DJ and a small bar. The music is spearheaded by DJ Tony who plays a mix of electro, break-beats and house but really gets the crowd going with a genre that is loved by many here –

new-wave '80s remixes and popular '90s dance classics. Dress well to get in here and prepare to drink and dance to loud and somewhat cheesy tunes, and you'll definitely have a good time.

Moloko, Monnot Street, Achrafieh
Tel: 01 755 853
Open: 8pm–2am daily

Moloko is a relatively simple bar and lounge located in a court-yard of about six bars just off Monnot Street. The courtyard contains three old stone buildings that have been revamped and rebuilt, and Moloko is one of these. The bar's simplicity is what makes it the perfect tonic to the rowdier drinking holes along the strip. In the summer, when it's hot, the bar spills out into the yard and is packed with chilled drinkers – or those who've failed to impress the other bars here. Moloko is the kind of place that sweeps everyone up. The music is good, a mix of hip-hop, pop and rock, and the people friendly. A TV screens the ever-popular football and basketball games and beers can be bought on tap for that genuine sports-fan feel. Because of the non-existent door policy the bar can become full of teenagers, but it's still worth a look.

Pacifico, Monnot Street, Achrafieh
Tel: 01 204 446
Open: 6pm–1am daily

The first, oldest and still most popular bar in the Monnot and arguably Beirut, Pacifico boasts a Mexican theme and menu, and the best barmen in town – see Johnny and Tony for details. Divided into a bar and restaurant with an outdoor terrace, Pacifico is one of those places where you need to make reservations (unless you want to squeeze up against the bar). Painted in a pale yellow to give off that sort of Latin American colonial feel, and with Michel, Camille and Steve's trademark ceiling fans – the same exists in Dragonfly – Pacifico is about two things – the cocktails and the atmosphere. An older crowd of well-healed Beirutis is meshed with wandering travellers, diplomats and journalists, all of whom know it's the place to be. With service to match the atmosphere, expect to be tipping high. The music ranges from Cuban to jazz and Afro-Latin, making Pacifico the place to go before you hit the clubs.

Shah Lounge, St Joseph University Street, Achrafieh
Tel: 01 330 033 www.ghiaholding.com
Open: 8pm–3am daily

A bar, restaurant or live music lounge? Shah Lounge is a little bit of everything very. A pleasant take on a typical Arabic nightclub, it is deeply oriental in style, with lush comfortable seating and a lot of space. In one corner the bar is a resting-place to watch the nightly bands performing Arabic pop and fusion tunes. An older crowd is more elite than usual, and all are smartly dressed with money in their pockets, but everyone is still hugely friendly. Once the food – a *mezze* of Lebanese and Mediterranean cuisine – is served and drinks arrive by the bottle, Shah Lounge takes on a life of its own, with everyone partying in true Lebanese style – the ladies seductively shake their behinds while the men circle around them clapping. Beirut's starlets *du jour* are known to turn up and perform a few impromptu numbers. All in all a little like London's famous Momo's.

Sky Bar, Palm Beach Hotel, Ain el Mreisseh, Downtown
Tel: 01 372 000
Open: 8pm–3am daily during summer

Sky Bar is one of the most exclusive bars in town, occupying two floors on top of the Palm Beach Hotel on Beirut's Corniche seafront, and serving amazing cocktails to a young and beautiful crowd. All very Fashion TV, with an accompaniment of mainly lounge and trip-hop music with some local Arabic tunes thrown in. The design is simple, with two bars on each level and wooden slats for a floor; low cream cushions are arranged as seats and sofas around the rooftop pool, all looking out over the marina towards the Chouf mountains in the distance. This is Beirut summer luxury – the Sky Bar is all about decadence and pure indulgence, helped along by sensational caipirinhas and mojitos. As the night goes on, everyone ends up dancing around the pool and occasionally peeling off their clothes and taking a dip. The door policy can be pretty rigid, so dress properly and if in doubt try making a reservation.

Starlet, Azarieh Building, Riad el Solh Street, Downtown
Tel: 03 555 695
Open: 10pm–3am daily

Of the few bars in downtown to have made the grade for *Hg2 Beirut*, Starlet is one of the best. Located on the second floor of an office building, it looks out over the main drag of Maarad Street, and aims to attract wealthy Arab tourists from the Gulf as well as the local glitterati (as the name 'Starlet' suggests). The concept is everyone's a star, so getting in may require you to sweet-talk the security. All in white, the central bar is the main feature with tables and chairs liberally scattered around. For us the best reason to come here was not the commercial music or

even the crowd, but the exquisite absinthe shots that really kick-start oblivion. Although relatively expensive, Starlet is worth a visit simply for the fun of being swept away in true Arabic glam style.

Time Out (La Closerie), Lebanon Street, Achrafieh
Tel: 01 331 938
Open: 7pm–2am daily

One of East Beirut's calmer bars, Time Out has been decked out like the living room of a quiet English country house. Consequently, the crowd is slightly older and attracts plenty of cigar-smokers and those in search of an intimate chat. Built inside an old Achrafieh house, Time Out has been around for years and occupies two levels, with a wide-open terrace for the summer months. A good selection of imported whiskies, gins and vodkas are on hand to help wash down the food, which includes chicken brochettes, sushi and sashimi. But really Time Out is for chilling out, as the name suggests. There's no other place like it in Beirut; relaxing, and good for a romantic drink, it makes a great alternative to all the designer venues in town.

Torino Express, Rue Gouraud, Gemayzeh
Tel: 03 611 101
Open: 8am–2am daily

This Gemyazeh mainstay is without question one of best little bars in Beirut. An old picture-framing shop, it was one of the first bars to open in the neighbourhood in 2003, and one that saw the potential of the area. Small in size – a mere hole in the wall – Torino Express is a café by day, serving wonderful Italian espressos and paninis; at night it becomes a bar with DJs spinning records (from Nu-Wave Depeche Mode to Jungle Jazz) and accomplished mixologists serving up fantastic cocktails. Lebanese–German owner Andreas Boulos has created an atmosphere second to none – there are no pretensions and the crowd is here to have fun. An all-wood décor is interspersed with antique lamps and old photographs, while Boulos has made a point of retaining the original tiled floor and arched ceiling. Make sure to visit the bathroom: one of Torino's most original features, it's all mirrored tiles, funky toiletries and classical music – quite different from the main room.

Zinc, 37 Seifeddine El Khatib Street, Achrafieh
Tel: 01 612 612
Open: 9pm–3am daily

Zinc opened in 1997 in an old 1920s villa at the top of end of Monnot Street, and has been packing in crowds ever since. Feeling like a pasha's bedroom, the T-shaped space has a velvet-sofa lounge area facing large bay windows that lead out into a private canopied garden. Incredibly trendy, Zinc attracts an older,

Francophone crowd (though not exclusively so). It's known for its atmosphere – low lights reflect off the deep red-ochre walls covered with modern art and photographs, while a DJ spins a mix of popular favourites from the '60s to today. Be sure to notice the original Lebanese tiled floor and mosaic underside to the bar – both intriguing features. The beautiful crowd seem to canter their way through numerous bottles of champagne and sip the wonderful cocktails (prepared with serious vigour), only occasionally pausing to graze the fusion cuisine on offer. Smoky and crowded, Zinc remains a staple on the Lebanese scene. Dress to impress.

notes & updates...

snack...

'How do you take your coffee?' says the waitress to the Lebanese man at the table. 'As black as the devil and as sweet as a stolen kiss,' he replies.

From flirtation to conversation, in Beirut Lebanese coffee – or *ahweh* to be precise – is a culture unto itself. And as a result Beirut's cafés are numerous, from trendy and chic to simple sidewalk and neighbourhood Arabic; and they're found everywhere, from the elegance of the Corniche to the backstreets of Hamra.

What's it all about? In a society where lunches are long and dinners drawn out, and work usually stops by five in the afternoon, for most, drinking coffee and chatting is simply the way of things. *Ahweh* is part of Lebanese culture; children, adolescents, adults – and especially the elderly – all drink it without discrimination for breakfast, lunch and dinner. Lebanese coffee is actually similar to Turkish coffee but quite a bit stronger, thicker and often flavoured with cardamom or orange-blossom water.

The story goes that coffee was one of gifts of Allah to the Prophet Mohammed, sent via his messenger Gabriel to lift him up during a period of fatigue. The

Islamic cultures embraced coffee as a social habit around the 15th century, brought in along the desert trade routes from its native East Africa, across the Red Sea and into Arabia. Coffee has always been prized because it clearly encouraged the type of vigorous scholarly dialogue on which early Islam thrived. Today, it does the same for family debates and after dinner conversation.

A typical recipe for the kind of coffee you see old men drinking on the Corniche as they gamble over *tawleh* (backgammon), and as explained to us by the elderly women in Jouya, southern Lebanon, is as follows: As the coffee begins to rise up, take it off the stove and, once the bubbling recedes, return the *ahweh* to the heat and bring it back to the boil. Repeat this procedure three times. Consequently, you will get the maximum coffee flavour without over boiling. There should remain a thick sediment on the bottom of the pan and a darkish brown foam on the top.

Of course, *ahweh* isn't the only type of coffee you can drink in Beirut – there are numerous places serving lattes and espressos and flavoured coffees as well as tea – mint tea is another Lebanese dietary staple.

The best traditional cafés are the legendary Café Rawda on the Corniche, and Aweht Azzeiz (the Glass Café) in Gemayzeh, which is open 24 hours and perfect for early morning breakfast after the partying all night. Both of these cafés provide *narguilehs*, if you fancy going the whole hog and smoking a water pipe. Look out for the guys who come round with the hot coals and normally dressed traditionally; they are always glad to help, and give good smoking advice (remember to give them a tip). Also good are the Grand Café in downtown and Regusto in Hamra. No Lebanese café could survive without serving food, and nearly all of them produce dishes ranging from Lebanese *mezze* to sandwiches. So go on – indulge.

Amore Mio Café, 732 Plaza, Verdun Street, Verdun
Tel: 01 795 151
Open: 9am–midnight daily

Amore Mio is one of Beirut's more pretentious cafés. Located in the trendy Verdun shopping area, at the entrance to a building housing numerous boutique stores, Amore Mio is lively, garish and always full with people-watchers on the outdoor terrace. Specializing in iced coffees, teas and a range of food – including a

sushi bar on its second floor – Amore Mio caters to the local neighbourhood crowd of wealthy luxury apartment residents and high-end shoppers who fancy lunch or a quick drink.

Aweht Azzeiz, Gouraud Street, Gemyazeh
Tel: 01 580 817
Open: 24 hours daily

Without doubt one of the best traditional Arabic–Lebanese cafés in town, the Glass Café is so called for its huge windows on every side. Although refurbished in 2001, it has been around for many years serving good, cheap Lebanese food and *ahweh* all day and all night. Popular with journalists, writers and old men who play backgammon and cards, smoke *narguileh* and drink *arak*, the Glass Café – a large square room with tables arranged orderly throughout – is totally authentic. The maître d', dressed in a tux, greets you as you walk in, finds you a suitable table and orders his waiters to take care of you. Great for playing or watching others play *tawle* or simply soaking up some of the traditional Lebanese atmosphere. Most evenings there is live music from an

oud player and *dbeki* drummer, and the older crowd dances around for hours. A true Beirut delight.

Bay Rock Café, General De Gaulle Avenue, Raouche, Corniche
Tel: 01 796 700
Open: 7am–2.30am daily

The Bay Rock Café is high up on the cliffs overlooking the famous Pigeon Rocks in the bay of Beirut. Hence, it does get touristy, but it's simply a beautiful spot with incredible views out over the Mediterranean. As well coffee, Bay Rock does fantastic

fresh lemonade, making it the perfect place to stop off along the Corniche after a stroll in the sunshine. The food is good – a typical menu of Lebanese *mezze* and fish – but expensive and because of the location more popular with foreigners than locals. Still, as seafront cafés go, Bay Rock takes the podium for its views alone.

Bread, Gouraud Street, Gemayzeh
Tel: 01 566 506
Open: 9am–midnight daily

One of the newer café–restaurants in Gemayzeh, Bread is a joint venture between local bakery Bread Republic and trendy restaurant Casablanca (see Eat). Found in one of the cavernous ground-floor cellar shop fronts of Gemayzeh's old buildings, Bread offers organic breakfasts and lunches, fresh bread, crois-sants and muffins baked on site, all within a warm and fashion-ably designed interior with cosy, sleek furniture. Somewhat artis-

tic in feel, with an air of urbane sophistication, it's a touch expen-sive and as such attracts many ladies-who-lunch, as well as local advertising execs. Nearly all the ingredients on the menu are organic, which partly explains the high price of some simple dishes, but the taste and the aromatic coffee more than makes up for that.

Café de Paris, Hamra Street, Hamra
Tel: 01 341 115
Open: 9am–8pm daily

Another old Hamra favourite of writers and artists, Café de
Paris is a stalwart Beirut café but one which, in recent years,
has become a little run down. This has been an indirect result
of the rebirth of downtown as a central focal point for Beirut.
With alfresco tables and chairs, and uniformed old waiters,
Café de Paris harks back to a Beirut and a Hamra of old, when
this street used to attract the cream of Beirut society. Today it
is popular with local shoppers and anyone wanting to
experience a little nostalgia. Serving coffees, teas and *croque-
monsieurs* in the way of snacks, Café de Paris is best for a quick
break from running errands around town or as somewhere quiet
to go if you just want to sip a tea and spend some time
alone.

Casper & Gambini, Maarad Street, Downtown
Tel: 01 983 666 www.casperandgambinis.com
Open: 9am–1am daily

One of the first restro-cafés to open in downtown with a firm
brand, Casper's has built its reputation on soft surroundings and
gourmet sandwiches, salads, desserts and coffees. A good vibe
exudes from a young crowd keen to lounge in the low-slung

leather chairs. Casper's two levels are decorated in dark brown mahogany with windows on two sides. From here you can survey the pedestrianized downtown café hubbub of Maarad Street, and the Roman ruins of the Cardo Maximus from a terrace. With plenty of coffee-table books on the bookshelves, non-invasive music and tasty food, Casper's lures in locals and chic Arab tourists from the Gulf dressed to impress. It is a haven from the louder and more commercial ventures on the rest of Maarad Street.

Chase, Sassine Square, Achrafieh
Tel: 01 202 390   www.chase.com.lb
Open 9am–11pm daily

Chase, located in this popular and traffic-filled square, is a Beirut institution that has been around for 27 years. But in keeping with

Beirut's ever-changing character, a recent refurbishment has made it very modern and Zen-like, rather impingeing on the old charm of the place. Still, you can't really go wrong here, with typical café food such as club sandwiches and *croque monsieurs* as well as more substantial dishes of grilled fish and meat, and a to-die-for chocolate mousse – all washed down with coffee of every description, from lattes to chocolate mocha specials and more. The front of the restaurant features silver aluminium siding and huge floor-to-ceiling windows looking out onto a wide sidewalk terrace and the everyday bustle of the square.

Le Coffee, Monnot Street, Achrafieh
Tel: 01 211 115
Open: 10am–midnight daily

Slapped up in a large new building in Monnot, directly opposite the now legendary Crystal nightclub, Le Coffee is a friendly café that has built on the popularity of the older Tribeca around the corner, giving this part of Achrafieh a new daytime lease of life. With black-and-white portraits of film stars and pop idols on the walls, and plenty of seating in deep velvet-covered chairs, Le

Coffee is almost the perfect place to relax – except, that is, for the lights, so bright that they create a sterile feel. The large menu comprises classic sandwiches, fried breakfasts and burgers, as well as a full complement of coffees. Le Coffee is an interesting

spot to people-watch, or just simply to come and browse through a selection of magazines from the collection of publications that lines the wall. The outside courtyard becomes a sun-trap on hazy summer days, while the interior provides succour from the winter chills. It certainly seems that this fashionable little café is here to stay.

De Prague, Makdissi Street, Hamra
Tel: 03 575 282
Open: 9am–2am daily

Opened in March 2005, De Prague brings to Hamra a café, bar and bookstore that is much needed in terms of vibe, style and quality. Formerly the Rose & Crown Pub, the large square space was gutted and refitted with simple sofas, antique furniture, candles and mirrors to give it a homey, casual feel. With student art on the walls, and fresh coffee and cakes from the kitchen, and a straightforward bar and DJs in the evenings, De Prague is the Hamra stop-off for a funky young scene. And it feels good. With luck, this should trigger a revitalization of the neighbourhood, as happened in Gemayzeh; we hope more such places will arrive soon. On Sundays the management shows art-house films on a

huge projector screen. Unsurprisingly the crowd is an arty one – primarily creatives and students generating an energetic atmosphere. The perfect place for lounging on long Sunday afternoons.

Grand Café, Saad Zarghoul Street, Downtown
Tel: 01 995 995
Open: 9am–1am daily

Grand Café is a swanky oriental café and eatery done out in traditional Ottoman style and located on both sides of a cobbled pedestrian street. All the waiters are dressed in traditional Lebanese manner, in a throwback to the years when the Ottomans held sway over the country, sporting wide baggy trousers tucked into boots and a fez on their head. Serving straightforward Lebanese food, sweets, coffee and tea, Grand Café is a place to grab a bite, drink a beer and either watch the shoppers go by, or simply gaze across the road at the stunning Sunni mosque, with its walls engraved with calligraphy. Always popular with visitors for its attentive staff and open vibe, it remains relatively cheap considering its location and its terrace. During the Islamic holy month of Ramadan, when Muslims fast during daylight hours, the place packs out at night, and it's often loud, too, with an Arabic band keeping the clientele entertained.

Henry's, Damascus Road, Achrafieh
Tel: 01 327 888
Open: 10am–10pm daily

A modern, no-frills café situated on a section of Damascus Road parallel to Monnot Street, Henry's is gracefully set back from the main drag in the ground floor of a rather nondescript office building. The menu varies from sandwiches, burgers and salads to old Lebanese favourites such as *shish taouk*, *kafta* and kebabs, all washed down with strong coffee. It has an easy atmosphere, which on weekday lunchtimes brings in the businessmen from nearby banks. The aroma of freshly ground coffee wafts onto the pavement, drawing customers in to make their choice of blends from around the world. Henry's is new and modern, and can be a good place to stop off if you've been hanging out in Achrafieh or shopping downtown.

● **Al Kahwa, Bliss Street, Hamra**
Tel: 01 362 232
Open: 9am–1am daily.

Located directly opposite the American University of Beirut, Al Kahwa is an Arabic café with large glass windows facing the street. Frequented by students, it does a good business in breakfasts, serving everything from local *kaak* bread to buffalo wings and ice cream. It also offers (of course) lots of black coffee and water pipes. One of the friendliest cafés in town, Al Kahwa straddles the fusion fence, catering to the large number of ex-pat foreign students and teachers at AUB as well as locals, but manages to provide consistently good food and a kicking atmosphere. The young crowd and reasonably priced and generously portioned food means that it's always a welcome pitstop.

Lina's, Saad Zarghoul Street, Downtown
Tel: 01 970 153
Open: 9am–midnight daily

Lina's now has a number of branches in Beirut including Hamra Street and the ABC shopping mall, but the most atmospheric has got to be the original space in downtown. A locally owned café and sandwich bar, Lina's has also managed to export the franchise to Paris and other Middle Eastern countries. With an overall green feel, Lina's is a good place to have a coffee and enjoy a gourmet sandwich or pastry. It's open and spacious, with two levels offering low tables and a range of papers and magazines. But perhaps best of all for those with laptops, Lina's offers wireless internet access. Just buy a card from the counter and you're off.

La Maison du Café Najjar, Foch Street, downtown
Tel: 01 998 800
Open: 10am–11pm daily

This chic café has a few other branches around the capital, but the one in Beirut's downtown is probably the best. La Maison du Café Najjar is chic and comfortable, with plenty of tables both inside and out. The Najjar family, purveyors of the local coffee brand *café Najjar*, are the driving force behind this stylish venue and it's abundantly clear that they take their business very seriously. The result is that every kind of coffee under the sun is available here (well, 50 in fact), including a wide range of authentic Arabic flavours. Offering light snacks and some good pastries, La Maison is set back from the more crowded Maarad Street, and is consequently much calmer. Because of its location and its marketing as high-end, La Maison is a touch more expensive than other cafés in the area, but you'll be happy to shoulder the extra expense to get away from the hurly burly of downtown.

Manara Palace Café, Manara, Corniche
Tel: 03 753 887
Open: 24 hours daily

Located right on the sea, the Manara Palace Café is always popular enough to warrant it opening all day and night. With an outdoor terrace as well as a large yet basic interior, the vibe is relaxed and pleasant during the day – perfect for snacks and

Turkish coffee flavoured with cardamom, as well as for taking in the sea air. During the night it becomes more upbeat, with a live Arabic group every evening from 10pm. But where Manara really

comes in handy is in the early morning after an all-night Beirut party binge. Come around 4 or 5am and eat – or continue to drink – to your heart's content while you watch the sunrise.

One Stop, Gouraud St, Gemyazeh
Tel: 01 562 898
Open: 9am–11pm daily

One of the newest cafés in Gemayzeh, located on the main drag of this once quiet street, One Stop is the pet project of local entrepreneur Alecco, and takes the form of a small, French-style bar/*tabac*. The food is average – it's not really somewhere you'd

choose come to eat – but the cakes and coffee make it worth 'one stop' if you find yourself in the neighbourhood. The interior is simple – all wooden furniture under maroon walls – but there's a typically Lebanese addition to the Parisian *tabac*: two TVs showing for the most part Fashion TV. Fun and buzzy, it's a great place for a short, sharp fix of caffeine.

Paul, Gouraud Street, Gemyazeh/Saifi
Tel: 01 582 222
Open: 9am–midnight daily

This high-class French café, bakery and patisserie does a thriving trade among the top end of society, and at lunchtime the place is full of cigar-smoking men, and women dressed in Yves Saint Laurent. Topping the fun of watching the crowd are the food, coffee and cakes, from éclairs to *pain d'epice*, all baked on site, and pretty much second to none. The décor is very Parisian with heavy wooden tables on tiled floors and a permanently popular outdoor terrace. The perfect place to indulge yourself any day of the week, Paul is what it is – amusing, loud, tasty and reassuringly expensive.

Place de L'Etoile, Place de L'Etoile, Downtown
Tel: 01 985 220
Open: 9am–midnight daily

Place de L'Etoile, named after the square it stands in, is directly opposite the Lebanese Parliament building in downtown, and is recently infamous as the last place the former Prime Minister Rafic Hariri sat for coffee before embarking on the fateful journey that saw him assassinated. One of Beirut's French-style cafés, it's set over two floors with expansive light and delicious food, including three different *plats du jour*. With a lovely outdoor area from which you can gaze over the two restored churches next to it, Place de L'Etoile is appealing as one of the quieter spots on

the downtown drag and the only place to stop in this central square. It can get busy, so service is sometimes a little slow, but sitting outside on a summer's evening is so pleasant no one will mind.

Rawda Café, Corniche, Manara
Tel: 01 743 348
Open: 8am–midnight daily

A legend among Beirut cafés, Rawda is an open-air square of concrete and grass directly on the seashore behind the famous Corniche Ferris wheel. It is a simple, traditional place with basic plastic chairs and tables, but it does a mean mint tea or Lebanese coffee and prides itself on its *narguilehs*. Rawda is perfect for Sunday mornings, general chill-outs or early evening chats watching the sunset. It's consistently popular among Beirut's film and literary clique as well as many Muslim and

Christian families spending quality time together. To be honest, the service is terrible but with about 100 tables to manage, it's to be expected and all taken in a spirit of fun. Rawda is an institution and shouldn't be missed, so pick a table and a water pipe and enjoy the sun and sea, local Beirut style.

Regusto, Hamra Street, Hamra
Tel: 01 752 571
Open: 11am–1am daily

Regusto is not much to speak of in terms of design: a simple, two-roomed space with a small bar, a TV for soccer and basketball games and a terrace for outdoor eating are located on the first floor of an office building in Hamra. The atmosphere is habitually rowdy and talk often turns political when the friendly

staff and customers all have an opinion. Run by the colourful Artur, known to his friends as 'Big Artur', Regusto serves a basic filter coffee, Liptons tea and *ahweh* as well as draught beer and cheap, filling Armenian food. But it's a Beirut institution known around town and enjoyed by many from 20-somethings to 40-somethings, and is entertaining for an early evening coffee or lunchtime snack, or just to have a laugh with the wisecracking staff.

Ristretto, Mahatma Gandhi Street, Hamra
Tel: 01 739 475
Open: 8am–8pm. Closed Sundays.

It's all about the espresso in Ristretto, a small café regularly packed with students from local universities AUB and LAU in Hamra. Having been around for a good few years, this simple American-style diner serves respectable pancakes and eggs for breakfast to an enthusiastic and loyal customer base that quickly packs out the few available seats. The vibe is constantly buzzing,

as is the coffee, and thus Ristretto becomes an ideal place to nurse your Friday night hangover before tackling anything quite as ambitious as the papers. The service is friendly, too, and if you're feeling like you haven't spoken English for a while you'll probably bump into some local students or professors only too willing to debate on local politics, history and the art of coffee.

Le Rouge, Gouraud Street, Gemayzeh

Tel: 01 442 366

Open: 9am–midnight daily

One of the friendliest cafés in town, Le Rouge not only serves fantastic coffee but also does a mean breakfast and has a decent selection of sandwiches and pizzas – all made with the freshest of ingredients. Popular with Beirutis, Rouge comes packed with a library of magazines and books, while the walls are adorned with literary quotations in French and English designed to distract you from your food. The atmosphere is unassuming and completely relaxed, and the waiters are suitably low-key, making Le Rouge a great place to drop in for a quick coffee or bite to eat. It does a thriving trade and gets quickly packed for lunch, so pop in around noon or not until 2pm to ensure you get a table.

Sydney's, Vendome Intercontinental Hotel, Ain el Mreisseh, downtown

Tel: 01 368 800

Open: 24 hours daily

Sydney's is the luxury café–bar for any taste at any time. With the feel of a British gentlemen's club, it is located high up on the roof of theIntercontinenal Le Vendômel with a conservatory and bar area. Sydney's is a hedonist's heaven, with deep leather chairs to sink into any time of day or night – but especially night.

The views are a delight – you can see all the way to the mountains above Jounieh bay in the north – and snacks and meals are available at any hour. On the whole, however, Sydney's functions more as a late-night bar when it fills with bejewelled Lebanese princesses and their wealthy boyfriends – making it even more fun. It's always a good place to go after a night on the tiles, but beware: it is easy to get stuck at Sydney's till dawn.

Tribeca, Abdel Wahab el Inglizi Street, Achrafieh
Tel: 01 339 123
Open: 9am–midnight daily

A New York style café à la *Friends*, Tribeca is an elegant little place in Abdel Wahab at the top of Monnot Street. Set in a restored Achrafieh house, it's airy and bright, with the work of

different local artists adorning the brick walls each month. Popular with the young, old and hip for its bagels and muffins, Tribeca, like its eponymous neighbourhood in the Big Apple, is a place to hang out and while away hours in fine company. Wide velvet sofas frame the oblong space filled with wooden tables, and chill-out music washes out over the assembled throng. It's a great brunch or breakfast haunt and a good place to spot the lovely Lebanese girls from the nearby Saint Joseph University.

Waterlemon, ABC Mall, Achrafieh
Tel: 01 212 888 www.h2o-lemon.com
Open: 10am–midnight daily

Waterlemon is one of those cafés you go to and stay in for an hour or two. It looks like a cross between something out of *Barbarella* and a grassy field. From its white plastic-fantastic sofas to the Chinese hanging basket seating to the glass globe light fixtures and coloured gel-filled place mats, this boutique juice bar and restaurant is all bright, shiny and spacey. The serious interior design was dreamed up by Georges Chidiac and four times a year a new seasonal theme is introduced which sees the napkins, walls, waiter's outfits and seat covers change colour. Waterlemon is fresh and funky, bright and breezy; it's a great place to stop for a fruit juice and a slice of cake while shopping in ABC mall, before you fight your way back through the masses that come here to buy, buy, buy.

Zaatar Wa Zeit, Rue Nasra, Sodeco, Achrafieh
Tel: 01 614 302
Open: 24 hours daily

At the lower end of the scale of post-club and bar café culture is Zaatar Wa Zeit, just at the top of Monnot Street, where most of the fall-out from an evening of drinking ends up on any given night. And they come because of the delicious *manaeesh* sandwiches at cheap prices. Squeezing into the booths that seat about 20 souls at best, Zaatar Wa Zeit has a high turnover and a lively atmosphere of young and old. It is perfect for meeting local Beirutis who may very well pick you up and take you on to a house party or another club afterwards, depending on the time of night. During the day it's the *manaeesh,* which can be stuffed with *falafel,* cheese, ham and other toppings, that makes Zaatar Wa Zeit a good, cheap eating option.

party...

To call Beirut party central of the Middle East would not be putting too fine a point on it. Fifteen years of civil war has left the populace with a need for escapism and indulgence – a need highlighted by the extravagant dining, drinking and decadent partying you'll find here.

In summer the action takes place on the beach, and the towns along the coast are bubbling with party spirit, but in Beirut the action runs all year round and all night long, as the glamorous and the hip strut from bar to bar before ending up in one of the city's electrifying nightclubs.

Many of the bars in town stay open into the small hours as their in-house DJs keep the young and the restless gyrating on the dance-floors. Nobody even thinks about hitting the clubs until about 2am, when the dancing begins in earnest and the spectacular sound systems reverberate through the die-hards until dawn.

The best of these are the legendary BO18 and the only truly mixed-gay club in Lebanon, Acid. Both play hard techno and tribal house most nights, but only really start hitting their stride from Wednesday to Sunday.

Arabic nightclubs are often ostentatiously luxurious, with wonderfully kitsch décor, and tend to attract wealthy suits and Arab tourists from the Gulf as well as the legendary Lebanese women, dressed up to the nines with their extended chests, large lips and layers of make-up. A musical assault on the ears comes from commercial pop and euro-house as well as techno-remixed Arabic *chaabi* pop – names such as Haifa Wehbe (a sort of Arab Britney Spears) and Georges Wassouf might be familiar. The best of these clubs are Crystal, where the champagne flows, and Taboo, where you might find girls eyeing your wallets rather than your looks. These places really have to be seen and sampled – they are something to behold, and decadent in a way you would never imagine. Often there's a popular local singer performing who dances round the club and plays with the audience. Try Cassino for this sort of thing.

Nightclubs don't tend to charge entrance fees but drinks will be relatively expensive. Your main problem, however, will be the door staff, who will make on-the-spot arbitrary and sometimes nonsensical decisions on who should be allowed in. Be sure to dress well and try not to turn up as a gang of men. Take on board local advice – it's always worthwhile.

During the summer numerous international DJs turn up to play special events in different venues – often converted exhibition halls or beach resorts, such as La Voile Bleu and Edde Sands (see Play) to the north and south of the capital.

In terms of live music there's a number of spaces that feature local jazz and rock groups – of these Bar Louie and The Blue Note Café are the most attractive, featuring the cream of the crop and often international jazz stars from New York and Europe.

Gambling is illegal in Lebanon apart from at the famous Casino du Liban, a very Monaco-style joint with live entertainment, cabarets and a restaurant overlooking Beirut and the Bay of Jounieh.

Acid, next to Futuroscope Exhibition Hall, Sin El Fil
Tel: 03 714 678
Open: 9pm–6am Fri, Sat

The only openly mixed-gay club in Beirut, Acid is famous for its
'90s raving vibe and attracts fans of hard house and techno,
young and old. The cavernous semi-circular club, with its huge

fresco of Indian deity Shiva above the long bar, is packed every
weekend. Women get in free while men, unusually for Beirut, pay
around $20 (which includes an open bar). Acid is loud and tends
to get jumping around 2am when the real party animals turn up
expecting heavy beats and floor-shaking sound. The sound system
is whopping and the laser light show impressive – they like their
lights in this town. The vibe is friendly and there are always after-
parties going on past dawn when the club shuts. This is one place
where young Lebanese really let loose on the huge dance-floor
and escape daily life. Expect to see all sorts of goings on in dark
corners and emerge blinking into daylight thoroughly blitzed.

BO18, Charles Malak Avenue, Karantina
Tel: 03 800 018
Open: 9pm–7am daily

The one Beirut nightclub that has truly attained worldwide fame is the legendary BO18. Designed by avant-garde architect Bernard Khoury, BO, as it is affectionately known, is located, rather morbidly, on the site of a brutal wartime massacre in Karantina. What makes BO18 so special is its design and the decadent, crazy, debauched vibe that drives it. It all happens in a small, box-shaped underground room – descend the stairs into the dark, bumping club where the music is hard techno and tribal house and the girls are wearing little more than heels and miniskirts. At the far end vampyric seats line the long bar, while the rest of the space is decked out with a number of low tables – each morbidly adorned with the image of a dead film or music legend. There is no real dance-floor – each seat closes down into

a bench to dance on. When the vibe from the mixed-age crowd gets suitably hot and sweaty, that's the cue for BO18's *pièce de resistance* – the mirrored roof opens up to reveal the star-spangled sky. Be sure to dress up and have a girl on your arm or alternatively pull up in a Porsche or you won't get in.

Buddha Bar, Asseily Building, Riad El Solh Square, Downtown
Tel: 01 993 199
Open: 9pm–4am. Closed Mondays.

Beirut's version of the famous Parisian nightclub is same-same but bigger. Set over three floors in the interior of one of down-town's rather ominous-looking banking buildings, it gives little indication that it's actually there at all – only the black grated doors and snazzy cars pulling up outside give it away. The first-

floor restaurant features Asian cuisine, while the second and third floors are bars – the upper one gets wild and dance-crazy from midnight. The décor is Asian hip fashion, with golden walls and little Buddha statues in alcoves. The red, blue and gold satin chairs surround the main event – the huge dominant golden Buddha statue presiding over its domain in the centre of the club. The mainly commercial house music and Arabic beats attract a rather pretentious crowd. It gets pretty packed but because of its size Buddha Bar doesn't really feel full – which can be good or bad depending on your mood. Check it out, have some expensive drinks, and move on somewhere a little funkier.

Cassino, Corner of Sodeco Square, Damascus Road
Tel: 01 656 777
Open: 9pm–5am Thurs–Sun

Of all the Arabic music clubs in Beirut, Cassino has one of the most extravagant reputations. Built from scratch, the place is state-of-the-art and, like its name resembles a James Bond set with secret booths and soft sofas filled with glamorous lounging extras. Dress to impress here and look forward to experiencing

the legendary Beirut Arabic one-man (or one-woman) show, where a local singer plays a *dbeki* drum and electro keyboards and sings up-tempo Arabic pop, while the crowd join in and boogie on down. Well worth checking out to watch the exclusive clientele, all cigars and style. Be sure to call and reserve a table, otherwise you might find it tough to get in. Look out, too, for the massive bottles of champagne that go for thousands of dollars – and get transported from the bar direct to your table on an overhead pulley system. It's all about the money, honey.

Crystal, Monnot Street, Achrafieh
Tel: 01 332 523
Open: 10pm–4am daily

Crystal is Beirut's one club that is truly all about glitz, glam and money. The model-like women sport *de rigueur* Manolos while men resemble Arab versions of Tony Montana, aka Scarface. All appropriate, considering the club resembles the debauched Miami nightspot depicted in Brian de Palma's classic film. Located midway down Monnot Street, Crystal is decadent and dramatic, and built for debauched behaviour. The truly flash buy $3,000 Salmanazars of champagne, carried on a salver to your table spot-lit by a lull in music – a good way to announce a new swinging dick is in town. You can here at Crystal before the lights get lower and the music gets louder – techno Arabic pop and commercial classics – and then join everyone dancing on the

tables and chairs – literally everywhere. Prepare to look the part, spend some money and party with beautiful people. Crystal never seems to go out of fashion and during the summer it really goes mad – a sort of Lebanese Les Caves du Roi.

Element, Damascus Road, Achrafieh
Tel: 01 212 100
Open: 8.30pm–5am daily

Drawing in the capital's beautiful and wealthy clientele every night of the week, Element is one of Beirut's legendary clubs,

built from scratch in what looks like a concrete bunker and surrounded by green grass dotted with runway lights. Go early, sink into the soft couches and chairs and eat from a French fusion-food menu. Element really hits its stride later on in the evening, however. A dark hallway opens out into rectangular space with tables and couches on one side and the bar on the other. Early on the music is chilled out, but once the witching hour comes around it turns into commercial dance and house mixed with classic rock and sing-along classics. The crowd love it and get very drunk and high, ending up dancing on the tables, bar or any-where else there's space. The music is loud and the atmosphere dirty with much bumping and grinding, making Element a truly Beiruti clubbing experience – and that means an experience like no other.

Gallery, 11 Mar Maroun Street, Achrafieh
Tel: 03 898 389
Open: 9pm–3am Thurs–Sat

Gallery is a Beirut designer club built in an old two-storey tradi-tional stone Achrafieh building at the lower end of this bar-packed street. Fifty years ago Gallery was a hotel, and today the second floor remains, in rather stark contrast, a cheap hostel for Syrian migrant workers. Although it may seem odd to an outsider

that this funky space has sleeping construction-labourers above it, to Beirutis it's all part of the mixed bag that is the capital. The club itself is a square of a room with a bar stretching across one end, behind which the DJ, in a raised booth, plays mostly house and R&B. Opposite the bar are low-slung sofas, and at the far end a raised VIP section with a white curtain to cut off the glitterati from the riff-raff. The crowd, though, is casual and relaxed, which makes a nice change from the more upmarket spots around.

Mandaloun, behind Sodeco Square, Achrafieh
Tel: 01 611 311
Open: Closed Sundays and Mondays.

Located close to Zinc (see Drink), just behind Sodeco Square and a short walk from Monnot Street, Mandaloun was the first Arabic-style nightclub, opening in 2001 and starting a trend followed by the likes of Crystal. It's surrounded by greenery outside vast windows, and at night the lighting shining on them from outside changes colour, creating a dark, remote, spiritual feel. Inside the music is dominated by an Arabic one-man show; it's popular with a slightly older crowd but still bristling with atmos-

phere. Later on as it gets hectic and the music gets louder a stage area above the bar is made available for dancing, and, as is popular in many clubs, a giant projector screen descends from the ceiling to play pop and R&B video clips. Probably the highlight of Mandaloun, apart from the drinks, are the Saturday night special guests – mainly local Lebanese pop starlets, often bursting from their outfits and looking much like Shakira! Best to reserve in advance.

Rai, Monnot Street, Achrafieh
Tel: 01 338 822
Open: 11pm–5am. Closed Mondays.

Deep in a basement underneath Monnot Street lies Rai, Beirut's equivalent – in décor at least – of London's Momo's. An oriental lounge special, Rai is like a sultan's harem with enclosed sofas in

soft, earthy colours and arabesque calligraphic swirls. The music is commercial Latin, house and heavy R&B with badass oriental techno beats that the fashion-conscious and sexy crowd lap up. It's advisable to reserve in advance to guarantee entrance, which might well mean booking a table, but bear in mind that Rai does-n't get going until around midnight – and then things really start to happen. Popular with hen nights and often full of champagne corks popping and ladies dancing on the bar, here's partying at Beirut's most decadent. They do a great Cosmo cocktail and a something called a Rai Special – vodka, *manzana* and apple juice.

Taboo, Lazarieh Building, Downtown
Tel: 01 998 100
Open: 10pm–5am. Closed Sundays and Mondays.

Taboo is a beautifully decorated downtown club and restaurant that has been doing a booming business for the last two years. Lights are kept very low and the ceiling glitters with fibre-optic lights that continually change colour. Because of its location, Taboo, attracts a Gulf tourist clientele alongside its regulars, some who come early to eat and others who come late to

party. Dancing on the bar and on the tables is as encouraged as everywhere else, while the DJ spins an R&B/Arabic pop mix. Unfortunately some of the most gorgeous women hanging out at the bar are likely to be working and may only respond if you look the part. Taboo is a dark club where the night ends when the last client leaves and where the barmen work hard on their drinks – try the Dirty Martini! Again the security is selective and largely depends on how good you look – so be prepared for rejection and always remain polite.

Villa, Sodeco Square, Achrafieh
Tel: 03 090 606
Open: 9pm–4am Thurs–Sat

Opened in 2005, Villa is the latest Arabic/pop club to hit Beirut's scene, and is located in an old, formerly run-down villa in Sodeco Square. Following the traditional mould of Arabic clubs, the music is loud and drinks are bought by the bottle. Enter through grand old doors and find a triangular room of long sofas and a colourful bar stacked with bottles and champagne magnums. The DJ plays tunes from a corner in what resembles a priest's pulpit which, in conjunction with the faux stained-glass windows gives

Villa the feeling of a debauched church. The music is house and commercial pop with Arabic beats and rhythms mixed in, and although it offers little that's different, Villa is the in-place at the moment, mainly because in Beirut's fickle scene it is the latest to open up.

LIVE MUSIC

Bar Louie, Gouraud Street, Gemayzeh
Tel: 01 575 877 www.bar-louie.com
Open: 8pm–2am. Closed Mondays.

One of the venues that makes the Beirut neighbourhood of Gemayzeh what it is, Bar Louie opened up in 2004 when there

was just one other bar nearby, and helped to revolutionize the area. An alternative space with alternative music – jazz, soul and bluegrass – and an alternative menu of Spanish *tapas* and cocktails, it typifies this part of town. It's a relaxed funky venue, so downbeat and low-key it could be an urban underground joint in Amsterdam rather than Beirut. Bar Louie's long rectangular shape filled with wood tables and soft red couches is topped off by an old-school Beirut vaulted stone ceiling reminiscent of a wine cellar. Once every couple of months Najib, the owner, will bring in top-name international performers to play. With a monopoly it owes to its unique style, it attracts a good crowd that's into the music – which makes it all the more worthwhile.

Blue Note, Makhoul Street, Hamra
Tel: 01 743 857 www.bluenotecafe.com
Open: 8pm–1am daily

Beirut's oldest and best jazz club is Hamra's Blue Note. Every night a live band of mostly local musicians plays blues, jazz, funk or Latin. The small restaurant–bar serves delicious Lebanese and

burgers. With photographs of jazz legends and all the international performers who have come to play here displayed on the walls, Blue Note is a friendly, relaxed place that really hits its stride when foreign jazz musicians turn up in town for a two-week stint. Boasting the likes of New York contemporary saxophone great Sonny Fortune and Chicago blues guitar legend

Eddie King as just some of the guests who have graced the club, Blue Note is probably the best venue for classic live jazz in town. And owner Khaled Nazha makes sure you feel welcome. A generally older Lebanese crowd particularly appreciates the blues and regularly ends up at Blue Note.

Music Hall, Starco Building, Downtown
Tel: 03 807 555
Open: 9pm–3am Thursday–Saturday.

Music Hall is one of the few places in Beirut where you can watch six or seven bands in one night as you eat a luscious dinner and drink bottles of blue-label alcohol. Formerly the Starco

Cinema, the space was taken over in late 2003 by record-label owner and music entrepreneur Michel Elefteriades, who created a sort of cabaret-show environment. A huge bar at the top overlooks the stage at the far end, with descending levels of sofas and tables, and seating beneath it. Each night features around six different acts: perhaps legendary Lebanese–Arabic singers Tony Hanna and his Gypsy Band or the octogenarian *tarab* queen Nahawand, the Palestinian Chehade Brothers, playing their mix of *oud* and gypsy funk, or the extremely camp Lebanese male belly-dancer Mosbah. Music Hall is packed with people of all ages who are up for a night of original and different music and performance. Although it gets cheesy at times, the atmosphere is always fun.

Nova, Sin El Fil Roundabout, Sin El Fil
Tel: 03 713 566
Open: 4pm–2am daily

One of Beirut's most popular live music venues, Nova is tucked away in an up-and-coming neighbourhood just outside central Beirut. Designed like an American roadhouse, it's large, with pool tables, basic tables and chairs, a bar and a stage where local rock and punk bands strut their stuff three or four times a week. The young crowd are into their music, so when a group such as local stars The Kordz play, they go wild. Bands usually perform a selection of their own tunes as well as covers. The drinks are cheap and the vibe incredibly up-for-it. During the week there are often opportunities to jam, so if you fancy a beer and stepping up to play some Hendrix riffs, Nova is your place. It makes a good appetizer for a big night out at nearby club Acid; but if you don't like rock, you won't like Nova.

CASINOS

Casino Du Liban, Jounieh
Tel: 09 855 888 www.cdl.com.lb
Open: midday–5am daily

Casino du Liban is the only legal casino in Lebanon. Located high up overlooking the Bay of Jounieh, this is gambling

Mediterranean-style. The legendary casino has a long history of glamour behind it, with icons such as Richard Burton and Elizabeth Taylor gambling the night away in the '60s when Lebanon was a holiday hideaway for the European jet-set – and today it retains much of that '60s style. As well as four major gaming rooms (the first of which opens at 5pm), there is a slot-machine area, a theatre, a banqueting hall and a Moulin Rouge style dance-show club. The dress code is suit and tie for men and formal dress for women, and you have to be 21 or over to get in. All major currencies and credit cards are accepted, but make sure you have identification on you. Getting there is not hard – it's a 20-minute taxi ride up the highway to the north.

ADULT ENTERTAINMENT

In Beirut there is not too much on offer in this department. In fact, Lebanon, being a Middle Eastern country, has no strip clubs (although it has plenty of prostitutes). Rather it has what are called 'Super Night Clubs', where many Eastern European and Russian girls work on three- to six-month contracts as dancers. Here you go and buy expensive drinks for ladies to your liking to sit and chat with you. If they like you and you spend enough cash in the club you can meet them the following day for lunch and maybe more.

The most worthwhile of these clubs are located in Jounieh and Maalmeltein just north of Beirut, and the best, or rather the least tacky, are Excalibur and Tiffany's. Excalibur is located deep in the underground of a building in Maalmetein, while Tiffany's is in a building in the nearby neighbourhood of Kaslik. No need to call in advance, but it might be worth it at weekends. But be pre-pared to spend hundreds of dollars if you want to get anywhere.

Excalibur, Maameltein Highway, Ghazir, Jounieh
Tel: 09 031 042 www.excaliburshow.co.lb

Tiffany's Club, Kaslik, Jounieh
Tel: 09 215 515 www.tiffanysclub.com

culture...

Beirut lives and breathes culture – in its tri-lingual population, in its numerous mosques and churches, and in its many art galleries and international music festivals within and outside of the capital. If you want it, you can find it.

The best way to get acquainted with the city's sights is on foot, either by walking up and down the Corniche or window-shopping and café-hopping the rebuilt downtown. When you feel more adventurous, wander the backstreets of Achrefieh and Gemazyeh.

The famous Pigeon Rocks, carved out of the cliffs and jutting up from the turquoise-blue sea, are a wonderful sight – especially when contrasted with the towering concrete shell of the former Holiday Inn hotel, ravaged by the war but still standing tall over the city like a familiar scar. There aren't many parks or areas of green, but the sea more than compensates for that.

In terms of museums, there's not a lot – both the National Museum, with its collection of antiquities, and the Sursock Musuem are well worth a look. On a more contemporary note, Beirut is also home to a number of local and regional artists who take their inspirations from the city, from the past, from their religion or from regional politics. Most can be found in the town's bars and eateries, chatting and working away. There are galleries and exhibition spaces

that show their work, but – as many local intellectuals argue – not enough, considering there is not even a national gallery to house the wealth of Lebanon's 200-year-old sculpting and painting tradition. Still, if you want to enjoy what is on show, the best places are Espace SD Gallery in Gemayzeh, Agial in Hamra, Art Lounge in Karantina and Janine Rubeiz in Raouche.

Solidere, the reconstruction company primarily responsible for the rebuilding of central Beirut, often holds open-air photography exhibitions in Place de l'Etoile and Martyr's Square throughout the year.

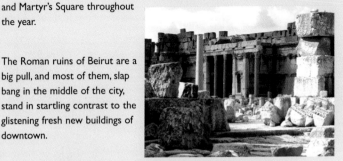

The Roman ruins of Beirut are a big pull, and most of them, slap bang in the middle of the city, stand in startling contrast to the glistening fresh new buildings of downtown.

Perhaps the most effective examples of cultural activity in Lebanon are the summer music festivals. The French Cultural Mission organizes a street festival of local and foreign bands ('La Fête de La Musique') once a year in June; and in 2004 the first Beirut Jazz Festival was held in the city's marina, next to the St Georges Yacht Club.

The best festivals occur in June, July, August and September outside Beirut in the picturesque village of Beiteddine, the Chouf Mountains, the ancient temples of Baalbek, the Crusader citadel at Byblos and the reconstructed Roman amphitheatre at Zouk Mikael. Famous international artists from James Brown to Massive Attack have all played at these festivals, which continue to go from strength to strength and are well worth timing your visit for.

Come October, the town's film festivals get into swing and include the Beirut International Film Festival, which shows local, regional and international features, and the Docudays Festival that brings cutting-edge political and investigative documentaries from the Arab world and beyond.

American University of Beirut/AUB Museum, Bliss Street, Hamra

Tel: 01 340 549   www.aub.edu

This famous university, built on a hill overlooking the sea, is one of the greenest and lushest locations in the city. It's a beautiful and relaxing place to wander around and enjoy the old buildings, which date back 150 years. The campus is open to the public and

certainly worth a few hours of your time. The university's archaeological museum was founded in 1868 and features a collection of Lebanese and Arabic artefacts and coins from the Stone Age onwards. There is also a selection of pottery and terracotta statuettes, and lectures are given throughout the year on a range of subjects.

Archaeological Remains, Downtown

After the war ended in 1991, the reconstruction process unearthed a huge number of Roman ruins, which make beautiful viewing when you're walking around the downtown area. Underneath the government offices housed in the Grand Serail, a vast restored Ottoman building, lie Beirut's ancient baths and a lush garden, while at numerous points in the area there stand remnants of the Roman city walls and streets. Look out also for the Cardo Maximus, a former Roman market with its grand pil-

lars sandwiched between the cafés of downtown and the Mohammed El Amine mosque.

Churches and Mosques, Downtown

The Beirut central downtown area contains an incredible number of churches and mosques – there are at least 30 in a space the size of the City of London – and the sound of church bells

and the call to prayer compete with each other in a cacophony of sound. Of different architectural styles and belonging to different religions, most of these were partly (or thoroughly) destroyed during the war but all have been restored and rebuilt.

All are of interest, but in particular look out for:

Al-Omari Sunni Mosque, Weygand Street, Downtown

Originally the Church of St John the Baptist of the Knights Hospitallers, but converted to a mosque in 1291.

St George's Maronite Cathedral, Riad El Solh Street, Downtown

St George's dates back to the Crusades.

Jewish Synagogue, Wadi Abou Jamil Street, Downtown

There is also the beautiful ruin of the only synagogue to exist in Beirut, harking back to the time before the Israeli invasion, when most Lebanese Jews fled the country.

The Corniche

A walk down along the seafront Corniche – amidst local families, roller-bladers, walkers and young, amorous couples getting away from the watchful eyes of their parents – is must-do, especially on weekend afternoons. The wide pavement that comprises the Corniche stretches from the St George's Beach Club in Ain el Mreisseh all the way to the Pigeon Rocks.

The National Museum, Damascus Road and Museum Crossing, Achafieh
Tel: 01 612 298 www.beirutnationalmusuem.com
Open: 9am–5pm. Closed Mondays.

A neoclassical building, the National Museum houses a large and impressive collection of archaeological objects and statues charting the history of Lebanon through the ages. During the war the museum was situated in the no-man's-land of the Green Line, dividing the city, and many of the items on show had to be encased in concrete by the curators to protect them from the fighting and looting. Meticulously restored, the national museum is worth the cheap cover charge ($3), and it's easy to get to – just hail a taxi and say, 'madhaf' or 'musée'.

Pigeon Rocks, The Corniche, Raouche

The most famous natural feature in Beirut, Pigeon Rocks are these breathtaking, off-shore rock arches rising out of the sea. Luring crowds of sightseers every day, but especially at weekends, they offer views at sunset that are simply wonderful. It's also possible to walk down across the shore from the road and look up at the chalk cliffs from below, and you can get a side-on view of the rocks as well. During the summer months local fishermen will gladly take you on a tour of the numerous caves and inlets for a small fee.

Robert Mouawad Private Musuem, adjacent to the British Embassy and the Grand Serail, Downtown
Tel: 01 980 970
Open: by appointment only

This private museum is housed in what used to be the Henry Pharoan Palace, named after the late head of a prestigious Lebanese dynasty. Bought and restored by the wealthy Lebanese jeweller Robert Mouawad, the museum now houses ancient Arab artefacts such as swords, pottery and jewels and *objets d'art* col-

lected by Pharoan and Mouawad over many decades. The building itself is an architectural showcase much like London's famous Orient House, featuring grand rooms with mosaic and tile floors and old Damascene and Aleppo wood-panelling and ceilings.

Sursock Musuem, Sursock Street, Gemayzeh
Tel: 01 334 133
Open 10am–1pm and 4–7pm daily

Owned by the Sursock family, one of the most famous in Beirut, the Sursock Museum is a beautiful Italian-Lebanese style mansion with an interior featuring wood-panelling, marble floors and colourful stained-glass windows. Different rooms are decorated in different styles – Damascene and Ottoman – and contain permanent exhibits of ancient jars, pottery and icons. There are often temporary exhibitions of photography and contemporary art, but it's best to phone and see if there's one on when you're here.

EXCURSIONS

Baalbeck Ruins, Baalbeck
Open: 8.30am–sunset

A trip to the famous Roman ruins at Baalbeck in the Bekaa Valley on the Syrian border is a must-do. Among the most important preserved Roman sites of the Middle East, the temples are vast, extravagant and breathtaking to behold. Begun in the first century bc, the complex expanded during the Roman period of occupation to include monumental temples to Jupiter, Venus and Bacchus. The town of Baalbeck was a centre for insurgency during the civil war and is where many of the hostages were held outside of Beirut. As it's a minimum two-hour journey from Beirut over lush mountains and amazing agricultural land in the Bekaa, be sure to start your journey early and spend the whole day here. Entrance costs $8.

Byblos (Jbeil)

This is a relatively easy trip north – just half an hour on the road when there's no traffic – so you can either take a taxi or bus from the Port of Beirut bus station to this picturesque ancient coastal town, famous for its crusader castle ruins and Phoenician history. It's an easy day trip that will allow you to relax away from the bustling capital, eat wonderful fish, shop in the newly restored covered cobbled streets of the old town, or sunbathe at the nearby beach resorts of Edde Sands and La Voile Bleu.

Ksara Winery, Ksara
Tel: 08 813 495
Open: 9am–7pm (4pm winter). Closed Sundays in winter.

Wine fans, as many hedonists are, must visit the oldest and most famous of Lebanon's wineries in the Bekaa Valley, south of Zahle town. Originally the site of a medieval fortress, it has bountiful grapevines and amazing underground caves where the barrels of Ksara are stored and mature. There's a decent 45-minute tour of the caves detailing the history and wine-making process of Ksara. Again take a taxi from Beirut or hire a car and drive yourself, but try not to drink too much – there's plenty of tasting on offer.

FESTIVALS

Lebanon is well known in the Arab world for its music and film festivals. The music festivals are held in major cultural and historic towns throughout the country during the summer and feature world-class international and regional performers, while the film festivals take place in autumn in Beirut. Treats in recent years have included Sting, Elton John, Jimmy Cliff, Massive Attack, Placido Domingo and Ahmad Jamal. Not to be missed, these open-air gigs are big on atmosphere and talent. The festivals are:

Baalbeck Festival, Baalbeck, July–August
www.baalbeck.org.lb

Beiteddine Festival, Beiteddine Palace July–August
www.beiteddinefestival.org

Byblos Festival, Byblos, June
www.byblosfestival.org

LibanJazz Festival, Zouk Mikael, September
www.libanjazz.com

Beirut International Film Festival, October
www.beirutfilmfoundation.org

ART GALLERIES

Agial Art Gallery, Abdel Aziz Street, Hamra
Tel: 01 345 213 www.agialart.com
Open: 10am–6.30pm. Closed Sundays.

Owned by collector and art dealer Saleh Barakat, Agial contains
a wealth of information on Arab art and painting. Showing the
likes of Syrian genius Sabhan Adam and Iraqi innovator Shakir

Hassan Al Said, and with a new show every month, Agial is the place to go for Arab art.

Alice Mogabgab Gallery, Gouraud Street, Gemayzeh
Tel: 03 210 424 www.alicemogabgab.com
Open: 10am–midday and 2–6pm. Closed Sunday.

One of Gemayzeh's best galleries for local, regional and international art run by dealer and agent Alice Mogabgab. Stop by if you are in Gemayzeh.

Arab Image Foundation, Starco Building, Downtown
Tel: 01 361 373 www.fai.org.lb
Call for opening times

One of the most important cultural foundations in the Middle East, the AIF is building a superior archive of photographs from the region, including 19th-century studio portraits and 20th-century pictorial practices. The collection gives an amazing insight into life in the Arab world over the last 150 years, and is a must-visit.

Espace SD, S. Dagher Building, Avenue Charles Hélou, Gemayzeh
Tel: 01 563 114 www.espacesd.com
Open: 4–8pm. Closed Sundays.

Espace SD in Gemayzeh is arguably the best and biggest gallery for contemporary art in Beirut. Run by the talented Sandra Dagher and spread out over three floors of the Dagher Building overlooking Beirut port, the space has a new show from an Arab artist twice a month and is fully booked until 2006. The second and third floors contain locally crafted furniture and accessories,

and books and CDs from Lebanese and Arab authors and musicians, all for sale, as well as a small and pleasant café, useful if you fancy a cup of tea. Look out as well for the avant-garde film showings in the small cinema also housed in the gallery. Espace SD is the place to go to understand modern Lebanon through its art.

Janine Rubeiz Gallery, Majdalani Building, Raouche
Tel: 01 868 290 www.galeriejaninerubeiz.com
Open 9am–7pm daily

One of the oldest galleries in Beirut, run by the daughter of Janine Rubeiz, who was one of the originators of Lebanon's cultural scene in the '60s and '70s. Artists and writers gathered here to talk, create and argue over issues of the day. Today the gallery hosts numerous exhibitions of classic and contemporary Lebanese and Arab artists, and has a large store of famous local artists for sale.

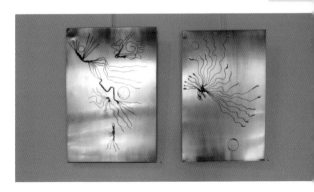

There are not many theatres in the capital, so most performances happen in the universities' audioriums; the more important ones are staged during the summer international arts festivals. The Monnot, Medina and Estral theatres are the main playhouses in Beirut, putting on diverse shows by local and regional groups mainly in French and Arabic. Call for details of shows when you visit. The theatres themselves are especially interesting – Medina and Estral are both housed in former underground cinemas in Hamra, and have a colourful history.

Monnot Theatre, Monnot Street, Achrafieh
Tel: 01 202 422

Medina Theatre, Saroulla Building, Hamra
Tel: 01 795 174

Estral Theatre, Hamra Street, Hamra
Tel: 03 614 355

CINEMA

Hollywood films are the mainstay of Lebanese distributors. Local films that do well in European film festivals often get a general release in Beirut, and regional films are played during the festivals, but no art-house cinema as such exists. The two big cinemas are:

Concorde Cinema, Concorde Plaza, Verdun Street
Tel: 01 738 439

Empire ABC, ABC Mall, Achrafieh
Tel: 01 209 208

CULTURAL INSTITUTES

There's a number of foreign cultural institutes in Beirut that often put on artistic, music and film events. Check their websites or call for details.

The British Council, Azzar Building, Sadat Street, Hamra
Tel: 01 740 123 www.britishcouncil.org/lebanon

French Cultural Institute, Damascus Road, Achrafieh
Tel: 01 615 859

Goethe Institute, Gideon Building, Bliss Street, Hamra
Tel: 01 740 524 www.goethe.de/beirut

Cervantes Institute, Maarad Street, Downtown,
Tel: 01 749 801 www.cervantes.es

notes & updates...

shop...

When it comes to shopping, Beirut is a paradise of clothes, gadgets, carpets, books, local antiques and souvenirs. This is a city of people that love to shop, especially for clothes, and almost every designer brand, from Gucci to Diesel, is represented here. Prices for labels, however, are roughly equivalent to those at home, so if you're looking for bargains you're unlikely to find them.

If it's the little and local items, or perhaps carpets and furnishings you're after, then you'll be fine in Beirut, even if you have to bargain for them. Alternatively if you have a penchant for *baclava* and other Middle Eastern delicacies, then you'll be in heaven.

For traditional Arab and Lebanese hand-made gowns and clothing, try Assyla in downtown Saifi village. All items are hand-made in a workshop in Baalbek; prices are steep, but the quality and design are exquisite. The best place for traditional local goods is the L'Artisan du Liban, located in Clemenceau, which is especially noted for backgammon sets and pashminas.

Verdun, in West Beirut, is the number-one shopping neighbourhood, packed full of boutiques, independent labels and trendy cafés. For European and American brands such as Morgan, Zara, Armani and DKNY, Verdun is the place to be. Downtown has also developed as an exclusive shopping area in recent years. In

the pedestrianized, cobbled streets, riddled with open-air cafés, you can find Gucci, Timberland, Karen Millen, Versace *et al.* vying for the best windows. And there is also Aishti, Beirut's answer to Harvey Nichols, full of only the smartest brands – if a little pricey.

For an authentically local and cheap shopping experience. try the market held every Sunday morning in East Beirut next to the river. Here, if you get up early enough, you can find every type of antique, bric-à-brac, clothing, beads and food, amid a very local crowd. Remember to bargain, otherwise you'll be had.

For local arts and crafts, from mosaic-inlay trays, cutlery, leather goods, rugs, copper and brassware, to gold jewellery, pottery, antiques, embroidered linens and lace, Beirut's formerly happening district of Hamra in West Beirut remains the place to go. Shops such as L'Artisan du Liban and little backstreet stores offer all of the above for reasonable prices.

If you've come yearning for a truly traditional and original shopping experience in the form of the ancient covered souqs, you won't find them in Beirut – all were destroyed during the war and have yet to be rebuilt. But you can find them, for those who are more adventurous, in Lebanon's other major cities – Saida in the south and Tripoli in the north. Here you will find wares from all over the region, including jewellery, cheap CDs, clothing, and food and drink.

Beirut's primary mall contains the ABC department store, housing everything from casual and formal wear to cosmetics and lingerie, as well as numerous other shops, cafés and a six-screen cinema. Spread over six levels, ABC is a feel-good shopping experience, with everything you could possibly want all under one roof. There is also a level full of jewellery stores which include the famous Swiss and Lebanese brands.

Aizone – high-end casual wear for men and women, including brands such as Diesel, Miu Miu and Armani; chic Lebanese store. Good for catching some European labels at cheaper prices than home.

Hallak – comprehensive selection of eyewear, including sunglasses from D&G, Gucci and Roberto Cavalli

Librairie Antoine – one of Beirut's best and most wide-ranging bookshops containing French, English and Arabic books as well as local and international newspapers

Mont Blanc – leather goods, pens, watches, belts and accessories from this famous luxury brand

Rectangle Jaune – Lebanese label specializing in casual and low-key menswear, good value shirts and jackets

Achrafieh, though not one of Beirut's primary shopping areas due to the stiff competition it faces from Hamra, Downtown and Verdun, nonetheless has a number of attractions for the committed shopper. Tucked away in the picturesque streets are numerous little independent antiques stores, furniture and design galleries crafts stores, jewellers and clothes shops featuring everything from locally made accessories to international designer labels.

C. Khairallah, Charles Malek Avenue – tribal and village hand-woven rugs from Iran, Turkey and Turkestan. Although it's a good idea to know your carpets before buying, Khairallah provides certificates of authenticity for each item.
La CD-Theque, Independence Street – the best music store in town, with a wide selection of local and Western music, DVDs and books

Milia M – exclusive young Lebanese designer with amazing creations for women. Perfect little black dresses.
Rabih Keyrouz, Lebanon Road – haute couture evening and wedding gowns from this locally based Lebanese designer who will takes orders and makes personalized creations
Sarah's Bag – hand-made selection of unique handbags. Colourful and individual.

This is Beirut's neighbourhood of antiques, vintage furniture and ancient lamps. It's a real market area with cavernous shops and plenty to gawk at, and you can take things to be mended here, too. A good place to wander around even if you're not buying – just grab a taxi and say 'Basta!'.

BHV Shopping Centre, Jnah – famous French department store housing a wide range of home furnishings, appliances, clothing and computers. Good if you are looking for well-priced items from non-designer brands.

As well as being the hub of central Beirut's café and restaurant life, the beautiful, pre-war sandstone buildings at the heart of the city house numerous boutique stores, primarily clothing and exclusive jewellery stores. The majority of stores house international brands. Downtown is a beautiful area of wide cobbled streets; it is a fantastic place to wander through, while away time at a café or spend that holiday cash.

Adidas – the Adidas concept store carries the brand new collections of footwear and sports clothing
Aishti – Beirut's answer to Harvey Nichols, Aishti is a four-storey designer shopping centre in downtown's exclusive bou-

tique area, housing exclusive top-line clothes labels, cosmetics, handbags and sunglasses. Housed in a beautifully restored building that had been all but destroyed during the war, Aishti has a great brasserie restaurant on the top floor.

Boss – all things Boss: the Black Label line for sophisticated style and the Orange Label line for casual wear

Conbipel – the Italian equivalent of Zara, Conbipel is a large glass-fronted store with value-for-money men's and women's clothing.

Elie Saab, Bab Idris – world-famous Lebanese fashion designer has recently installed his Lebanese headquarters in a brand new box-like building in this residential area of downtown. The creations of the man who dresses Hollywood film stars such as Halle Berry are expensive.

If – an original Beirut label, If is also full of elegant clothes for men and women and includes labels such as Ghost, Yohji Yamamoto and Dries Van Noten

Karen Millen – exclusive designer fashion label for women

Klass – mobile phone and accessories store. The best place to buy pay-as-you-go.

Morgan – stylish and trendy women's wear from this French label

Sportstown – all items Nike at Sportstown, for that sporting emergency

Virgin Megastore – books, CDs, comics and even a rooftop restaurant with stunning views over the sea and downtown (only open in summer).

Hamra was once the centre of Beirut life in the 1960s, and was packed with cinemas, bars and cafés. Today it has lost much of its allure and custom to the rebuilt downtown area, but many local stores, make-up shops and bookshops still remain. The main Hamra high street has recently been paved with cobblestones in an effort to reinvigorate it, and it's a pleasant place to be.

Artisan du Liban, Clemenceau – the shop to go to for all traditional Lebanese arts and crafts. It has everything – handmade oriental furniture, cutlery from the town of Jezzine, silver jewellery from the town of Rachaya, *abayas*, copper, linens, pottery, blown glass and backgammon sets.

House of Mars, Hamra – Lebanese-run store full of hippie-chic T-shirts, lamp shades and badges. Also a safe and hygienic spot to get tattoos and piercings.

Jack and Jones, Hamra – own-brand casual and sportswear for men, including a large selection of jeans and trainers

Maison des Soldes, Hamra – decent bargain store for major Italian clothing labels

Moustapha Laban, Sadat Street – large store selling perfumes and cosmetics from brands that include Sisley and Calvin Klein

Opened in December 2004, this intimate neighbourhood of small streets in a residential area of downtown just off Martyr's Square is Beirut's answer to Portobello Market, with plenty of galleries, design, furniture and fashion stores, and is well worth a visit. All the stores and galleries in the village are local or region-al. It's a good spot to wander around on a hot day and look at the local art and design.

Assyla – specializes in traditional Lebanese outfits: *arbeyas*, shawls, shirts and dresses, all embroidered in hand-dyed materi-als and brightly coloured. The original shop is in the town of Baalbek in the Bekaa Valley, but this new store in Saifi Village has everything.

Epreuve D'Artiste – Amal Traboulsi has been one of the most active patrons of Lebanese art for over 20 years. In that time her gallery has featured prominent old and modern Lebanese and regional artists in varied genres. The gallery has moved locations three times but is now hopefully permanently located in downtown's new arts quarter Saifi Village. The gallery itself fea-tures numerous works of art and sculpture, as well as home designer accessories.

Milia M – One of Beirut's most brilliant and recognized young fashion designers, this is Milia's first little shop, . A boutique designer, she sells internationally and does a lot of work in

Istanbul. Her clothes for women are all individual pieces and intimate with flowing lines and shapes designed to make one look both elegant and sexy.

Johnny Farah – For all your trendy leather accessories Johnny Farah is your man. His small shop specializes in everything from clothes and book covers to wallets and watch straps. Anything you want for the home he'll design on commission.

Nada Debs – Nada Debs has received a huge amount of local and international press over the last 5 years. Her designs for tables, chairs, lamps and jewellery are in high demand today and her new store provides the perfect showcase for her talent.

Plum – A contemporary fashion store featuring independent international designers and labels from New York and Europe. The funky interior design promises a very different shopping experience. But check it out for yourself.

SOUQ AL BARGHOUT, MARTYR'S SQUARE

This covered market of antiques and artisana takes place every August in Beirut's Martyr's Square, and is in its 23rd year. This souq is a massive flea market of furniture, carpets, antiques, porcelain, jewellery, paintings and *objets d'art*, and is full of bargains if you are prepared to haggle.

VERDUN

West Beirut's answer to downtown, this small neighbourhood is

packed with boutique stores full of everything from clothes to furniture to gadgets. A popular hang-out for society's finest with time to shop and chat. The mall in the basement of the Dunes Plaza also has a cinema and is always full of teenagers and kids.

Mango, Assaf Centre – popular Spanish franchise featuring day and evening collections for women

Nicolas Jebran – popular Lebanese designer with a haute couture and ready-to-wear line

Pull & Bear, Verdun Building – inexpensive, good quality, trendy clothes for fashionable men and women. It's the younger brother of Zara and features the brands Xdye and Sickonineteen.

Zara, Concorde Plaza – solid and reliable, reasonably priced clothes for men with lots of panache

play...

Beirut is a city of food and drink, places of worship, sun, traffic and often pollution. It can, if you're plan on staying a while, get just a little bit urban and stifling.

Although there's a number of ways to unwind within the city – from some of the top hotel spas to the beach clubs of the Corniche – you can always get out of town and check out the some of the most beautiful Mediterranean resorts in The Levant, or visit the breathtaking mountains and beautiful valleys to the north or south.

During the winter season – generally late December to the end of February – the mountain heights of Faqra and Faraya, just an hour's drive from the centre of Beirut, or, for the more intrepid, the Cedars skiing resort about 4 hours away, are stunningly beautiful and a lot of fun. Skiing is cheap and accessible; you can easily travel to Faraya and back in a day; and although the slopes are not as good as the Alps, they're good enough, and fully equipped for ski-hire and snowmobiles.

During the summer the beach resorts are a must. Just half an hour north or south of Beirut you can find high- and low-end resorts that have sprung up in recent years. Most charge a $10 entry fee for the day and have pools, bars, restaurants and sandy beaches. The best spots are in Byblos to the north and Jiye to the south. Edde Sands and La Voile Bleu are more exclusive, while Atlas Paradise has simple stretches of sand and sea and a couple of recliners.

There are also hiking and tour companies that will take you on day trips into some of the most lush countryside in the Middle East – you'll get to see the Bekaa Valley and the Chouf mountains, the ancient Cedars of Lebanon and the country's plentiful rivers, where you can go kayaking and rafting. However, don't feel that you need to go with a group or an organized tour – car rental is cheap and the country easily small enough to explore by yourself (although driving here can be a videogame experience).

In Beirut itself there are a number of cycling shops that will rent you a bike and take you on a tour of the city. The best time for this is on Sundays when parts of the downtown area are blocked off from cars and make perfect biking territory.

Young Beirutis like their sports and there are basketball and small football courts all around the city. The best is Hoops in downtown, next to the Starco building. If you are into golf you can also enjoy a round of nine holes, or for shooting enthusiasts there's an impressive selection of handguns at the Magnum Shooting range.

Generally, Beirut is not a sports minded city, but if you are willing to travel outside the capital to the magnificent countryside you'll be well satisfied. It's the perfect antidote to all that rich food and late-night drinking.

Lebanon's beach resorts are either located in Beirut (where there's little sand) or about half an hour's drive out of the city (where there's lots). Byblos and Jiyeh are the best resorts on Lebanon's picturesque coastline. In Beirut itself there is only one sandy beach, the public beach at Ramlet el Baida, but unfortunately it's not well kept – it's dirty and lacks proper lifeguards. The best Beirut resort is the Sporting Club, a slab of concrete just beneath the Ferris wheel on the Corniche, with two salt water pools and plenty of sun recliners. La Plage is more exclusive but offers little more than Sporting for double the $5 entrance fee. Most of the city's hotels have pools that can be used for a daily fee by non-residents.

Atlas Beach, Jiyeh
Tel: 03 222 309

Atlas Beach is one of the more chilled beach clubs south of Beirut; it has none of the loud music and state-of-the-art facilities you'll find at La Voile Bleu or Edde Sands. If you looking to truly chill out for the day without noise pollution from jet-skis and inane social banter Atlas Beach is the place for you. Cheaper than the rest at $5.

Bamboo Bay, Jiyeh
Tel: 03 513 888
Open: 9am–8pm daily, May–October

Bamboo Bay is the equivalent of La Voile Bleu to the south of Beirut in the Jiyeh area. Arranged like a colonial or Thai resort this beach is a delight of grass, jacuzzis, a pool and golden sandy beaches, with an outlet of Beirut's legendary Italian restaurant La Posta providing the food. $10 will get you in.

Edde Sands, Byblos (Jbeil)
Tel: 09 546 666
Open: 9am–midnight daily, April–October

One of the most beautiful high-end resorts in Lebanon, Edde Sands has all the amenities you could want, from golden sandy beaches to grass plateaus to six swimming pools. Luxuriously covered beds on the beach bear reclining beauties admiring their beaus sailing and jet-skiing. There are two bars and a couple of restaurants, and the height of summer sees the place packed to the brim, an Ibiza-esque paradise with DJs spinning the decks from the early afternoon to late into the night. Entrance is $10. Take a cab for about $25 to Jbeil (or the bus for about $5) and you'll see the signs.

La Plage, Ain El Mreisseh, Beirut
Tel: 01 366 222
Open: 9am–7pm daily, May-October

This seaside pool is also know as Silicon Beach for the amount of beautiful women (and men) who turn up looking buff, sexy and incredibly manicured (and augmented). It's a good choice if you don't want to leave the city but it's not totally relaxing as you'll be distracted by the sights of the beautiful bodies and amusing tittle-tattle about the affairs of Beirut's society crowd. A changing room and towels are provided and entrance is $10.

Public Beach, Tyre
Open: all year round

Lebanon's southernmost city, famous for its archaeological ruins and rich history, has the best stretch of undeveloped beach in Lebanon. Part of the Tyre Nature Reserve, which means that development is forbidden, the beach is clean, the sand white and the sea a gorgeous green. Although services are kept to a minimum, at the back of the beach a long row of wooden huts is erected and taken down each season which provide drinks and food. A simply beautiful beach close to the city's ruins, which include Alexander the Great's monumental Arch, to make a relaxing and culturally stimulating day trip. Allow about 2 hours to get there and back, depending on traffic.

Sporting Club, Bain Militaire Street, Manara, Beirut
Tel: 01 742 481
Open: 9am–6pm daily

Sporting is Beirut's chilled beach resort, where you can relax in the sun for the day before crawling back to your hotel all tanned and beautiful. It has two pools and a plethora of restaurants, and even offers scuba-diving. Not much to look at – literally just a massive concrete promontory with two pools sunk into the middle surrounded by sun loungers – Sporting has a charm that the more avant-garde Beirutis seem to love. It'is well worth a trip on a sunny afternoon.

La Voile Bleu, Byblos (Jbeil)
Tel: 09 796 060
Open: 9am–midnight daily, April–October

Located right next to Edde Sands, La Voile Bleu is party central. Chill on the sandy beach or recline next to the luxurious pools, occasionally exploring the different bars raised on wood-decked platforms, where you can choose to lounge, tan or drink till you drop. It shares the same stretch of beach as Edde Sands. Cost is $10.

CYCLING

Beirut by Bike, Minet El Hosn, Downtown
Tel: 03 206 796

This is the main Beirut bike club where bikes can be hired for daily tours of the city. They are a good crew of people and will provide you with a guide if you wish, or maps, as well as the protective gear you'll need to face the city's onslaught of traffic. Biking enables you to see the city from a different perspective, but be aware that Lebanese drivers can be a little crazy and have little respect for cyclists – or pedestrians, for that matter.

If you want to learn to fly or can fly already, bear in mind that the airport is so close to the centre of town that it's almost a must to have a go. The Aero Club and Flying Carpet are certified flight clubs that will teach you to fly or take you sightseeing from the sky. Pleasure flights with the Aero Club will set you back around $100 for an hour if it's just you, or $250 for five people. Flying Carpet is slightly more reasonable at $35 per person.

Aero Club of Lebanon, Beirut International Airport
Tel: 03 370 928

Flying Carpet, Beirut International Airport
Tel: 03 682 255

The Golf Club, Jnah
Tel: 01 826 335

There is only one golf club in Beirut since it's not the most popular sport in this part of the world – hence it's relatively exclusive with a somewhat colonial atmosphere. Located near the airport, it is, however, one of the biggest stretches of green in the city with 18 decent holes. For those not so interested in rubbing the green, tennis, squash, a swimming pool and a billiards and bridge room are also on offer.

The Hippodrome, Museum Road, Madhaf, Mazraa
Open: 10am–4pm Sundays

For a great Sunday outing, try the horse races at the Beirut Hippodrome, located in a wide open space parallel to the French

Ambassador's residence. You can gamble on the horses and get stuck in with the passionate local crowd. Cheap and cheerful, and a good way to shift a hang-over after a Saturday night on the town.

OUTDOOR ADVENTURE

Blue sky, warm Mediterranean waters, fresh air, mountain peaks and the bracing chill of snow-fed rivers all make Lebanon a hiker's and nature lover's paradise. From the bird-rich coastal marshes and wetlands to the dramatic arboretums of Cedars, the country's rich ecosystem will delight any enthusiast. There is a number of companies that will organize tailor-made trips for a day, two days, weekends or longer. The most efficient and reliable are listed below.

Afqa Reserve, Mnaitra (north of Byblos)
Tel: 03 633 644 www.lareserve.com.lb

Afqa is located high up on Mount Lebanon north of Beirut, a lush plateau where all sorts of outdoor activities can be enjoyed by people of all ages and levels of experience. It's an amazing reserve where you can go for a day, or camp the night in solid canvas tents with bunks provided for you or in your own tent. Horse-riding, mountain-biking, hiking, caving, parasailing and archery are all on offer.

Cyclamen
Tel: 03 218 048 cyclamen@terra.net.lb

The best organization for mountain biking, Cyclamen will take you on trips in the remote Northern Bekaa Valley and more. Call for details, but prices for day trips including all meals and transport cost around $25. Prepare to get those leg muscles working.

Esprit Nomade
Tel: 09 635 294 www.esprit-nomade.com

Esprit Nomade organizes hiking trips, including coastal walks to the seaside treasures of North Lebanon. The drive to Enfe is about 2 hours, and the hike itself about 3 hours exploring salt marshes, monasteries and historical ruins. It's not overly arduous and is available to everyone. Any day trip with Esprit Nomade includes guides, breakfast and lunch, and all transport. A tour like this costs around $20 per person.

Exit to Nature
Tel: 03 985 066 www.exittonature.com

An experienced and well-organized company that will take you snowshoeing in the Cedars or teach you snowboarding in Faraya, with charges for a day ranging from $25 to $75 depending on the size of the group.

Lebanese Adventure
Tel: 03 360 027 www.lebanese-adventure.com

Lebanese Adventure has a range of activities and outings that include everything from mountain biking and caving to sailing and star-gazing.

Yellow Submarine, Beirut marina
Tel: 03 677 355

For something a little bit different try the Yellow Submarine, which floats in the sea around the Corniche. It's a funny yellow ship with an underwater viewing section that boasts a submarine view of the bottom. One-hour trips (on offer throughout the day) cost around $10.

SHOOTING

The Magnum Club, Mar Entanious Street, Hadath
Tel: 05 469 369
Open: 3–10pm daily

This private indoor shooting club is the place to learn how to shoot a handgun or alternatively practise your technique. It has three indoor shooting galleries with 22 shooting lanes. Charges are levied by lane and ammunition.

There are many health clubs and gyms in town as Beirutis like to look good for the summer months, when it's bare skin all around and beach-living galore. But when it comes to spas there are really only two that fit the true hedonist's bill. These are located in the luxury hotels Intercontinental Phoenicia and the Mövenpick. Unfortunately there are no functioning traditional hammams left in Lebanon, so it's all modern spa treatment instead.

Essential Spa and Health Club, Mövenpick Hotel, Raouche
Tel: 01 802 715

A 3,000sq metre spa and health club, this really is luxury relaxation at its finest. Offering a huge range of massages and treatments at reasonable prices, it has relaxation rooms, jet showers, steam rooms and saunas, and four swimming pools, both outdoor and in. Never very full, it makes for a tranquil escape from Beirut's urban sprawl.

The Spa, Intercontinental Phoenicia Hotel, Aie El Mreisseh
Tel: 01 369 100

The most lush and luxurious spa in town, the Phoenicia offers absolutely everything – but at a price. Balneotherapy and hydro massage, algo-therapy and presso-therapy are all on the menu. Or if you want aerobics, steam rooms, saunas, jet showers or just a facial, it's all here, in a split-level section of the hotel decked out in marble and mosaic. You will want to return here again and again to be totally pampered, and drain away the excesses of the night before. Day packages are available.

SKIING

SKIING

Lebanon is just as much a winter paradise as it is a summer one, with at least six resorts catering to skiers and snowboarders. If downhill action isn't your thing, the massive hinterland is perfect for cross-country skiing, snowshoeing and snowmobile adventures. The main resorts are listed below.

Cedars
Tel: 03 399 133

Located on Mount Makmel, to the north of Beirut, the Cedars is considered Lebanon's oldest resort, but a definite second in development and facilities to the closer Faraya. Named after Lebanon's national tree, of which there are still a few left on the mountainside, this resort is about 1,950m above sea level, with good snow depth for most of the season. The runs here are long, with lots of off-piste sections for the more adventurous skiers. The trip will take you at least 3–4 hours, and longer if the weather is bad. A day pass costs $17 on weekdays and $24 at weekends. It is a beautiful place and well worth a visit if you have time to spend a few days out of Beirut.

Faraya Mzaar
Tel: 09 341 502
Open: 8am–4pm daily, December–March

Faraya Mzaar (at an altitude of 1,850–2,465m) are the capital's nearest ski resorts – getting there is a easy cab ride from Beirut. It's sleepy most of the year, but good hiking is to be had in the summer and decent skiing from December to March. Faqra (tel: 01 257 220) is a private club in the town of Faraya – it's only accessible if you stay at the exclusive hotel. The Faraya Mzaar resort itself is probably the best equipped of Lebanon's ski destinations. The expansive lift system, decent annual snowfall and fantastic partying and après-ski facilities make it worth the trip even if you're not a fanatical skier. The alpine atmosphere extends to the plethora of fondue restaurants and even a mountain version of Beirut's legendary Crystal nightclub. The slopes are divided into three areas – Refuge, Jonction and Wardeh – but all are linked and cater for skiers of various levels of experience. The best hotel here is the Intercontinental Mzaar (09 340 100) located right beneath the slopes, but there are cheaper ones. An adult day pass in Faraya will set you back $17–25 weekdays and $28–45 at weekends. There are 17 lifts in total.

Laqlouq
Tel: 03 256 853

This is one of Lebanon's smaller ski resorts whose slopes cater mainly for beginners and intermediates. More advanced skiers will probably be unchallenged by the gentle pistes. At about 1,920m above sea level and 28km east of Jbeil, it's best for cross-country skiers and snowmobile fanatics. But it is cheaper than Faraya Mzaar at $20 for a day pass at weekends and only $10 during the week.

Zaarour
Tel: 04 310 010

The smallest ski resort in Lebanon, Zaarour is a beautiful spot. Located far north of Beirut, it is better for a weekend trip or extended stay than a day trip. A private club and an exclusive resort, it boasts spectacular views: the vista from Mount Sannine spans the whole of Lebanon. As it is a private club, it is advisable to call ahead to check availability and details.

notes & updates...

CLIMATE

In the summer Beirut is hot. The sun shines for months on end and it's easy to tan just walking down the street. From late May to early October temperatures reach the mid-30s and the air can become rather humid; from late October to December the temperatures settle in the early 20s; and from January to April it can dip below 20 degrees. It doesn't rain often, but when it does, usually December through March, the heavens really open up with intense thunder and lightning.

DANGERS

There is very little violent crime, and there's a conspicuous police and army presence on the streets. At worst, there may be the occasional motorcycle drive-by handbag snatching. Beirut is generally very safe for women, although – as anywhere – walking alone late at night in quiet streets is not recommended. Homosexuality is still technically illegal so the scene is primarily underground; public displays of affection are not recommended.

GETTING INTO TOWN

Getting into town from Beirut airport is relatively straightforward. There are numerous taxis as you walk outside the airport and the minimum fare for the short 20-minute journey to almost any neighbourhood is $15. If you have booked into one of the major hotels they can arrange a car for you in advance.

MONEY

The Lebanese currency is the lira, but US dollars are also widely used and are legal tender everywhere. The present rate of exchange is about £1=LL2,500, $1=LL1,500. There are numerous banks and plenty of ATMs so you should never be stuck for money, and all credit and debit cards are accepted.

NEWSPAPERS

The Guide, published in English, is probably the best source of information about the latest goings on in Beirut, and it also gives cinema and theatre listings. The *Agenda Culturel,* in French, is the best guide to arts, cultural and music events.

The only newspaper in English is *The Daily Star*, covering national and regional news and politics; it has a strong cultural section. Most foreign papers are available but usually a day after publication.

TAXIS

The most popular form of transport is the Lebanese Servis taxi, old white Mercedes that will pick you up from the side of the road. Most trips cost less than a dollar, if you are prepared to share, or some may charge about $5 to take you to a specific address. Alternatively there are numerous private cab firms which operate 24-hours a day and which will charge around $3–6 for journeys in and around Beirut. The ones we recommend are Safe Taxi on 01 337 344 and Queen Taxi on 01 545 442. Private taxis are safer and more comfortable than Servis, especially for women travelling alone at night.

TELEPHONES

The phone numbers in this book include the city code (01). The international code is +961, and for mobiles the prefix is 03. All numbers consist of six figures plus the city or mobile code. Make sure that your mobile telephone has the international roaming option switched on.

TIPPING

In bars leaving a tip will ensure that the barman notices you again, and sorts you out next time round. Standard rules apply – 10% for restaurants if the service is not included. Hotel bellboys and porters, as well as parking attendants, will always expect a minimum of LL3,000. There is no particular need to tip taxi drivers, although, again, feel free. Do bear in mind that the average wage in Lebanon is $200 a month.

VISAS

A visa is needed when entering Lebanon. It can either be attained from a Lebanese embassy prior to arrival, or – at the time of writing – can be bought at the airport on arrival, but do check as this can change at any moment.

index